I wonder - who was the
Freddie in your life?
All the best,
Tripp 6 May 09

P.S. Note Regent on the cover.
Yep, Angel Cabrera! How's
that for a little prophecy?

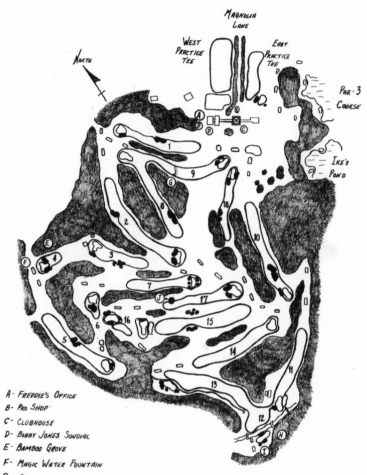

MAGNOLIA
LANE

WEST
PRACTICE
TEE

EAST
PRACTICE
TEE

North

PAR·3
COURSE

IKE'S
POND

A- FREDDIE'S OFFICE
B- PRO SHOP
C- CLUBHOUSE
D- BOBBY JONES SUNDIAL
E- BAMBOO GROVE
F- MAGIC WATER FOUNTAIN
G- ROBERTS RIDGE
H- SECRET LOBLOLLIES
I- INDIAN BURIAL GROUND
J- IKE'S TREE

FREDDIE & ME

FREDDIE & ME

Life Lessons from Freddie Bennett, Augusta National's Legendary Caddy Master

Tripp Bowden

SKYHORSE PUBLISHING

Skyhorse Publishing books may be purchased in bulk at special discounts for
sales promotion, corporate gifts, fundraising, or educational purposes. Special
editions can also be created to specifications. For details, contact Special Sales
Department, Skyhorse Publishing, 555 Eighth Avenue, Suite 903, New York,
NY 10018 or info@skyhorsepublishing.com.

www.skyhorsepublishing.com

10 9 8 7 6 5 4 3 2 1

Library of Congress Cataloging-in-Publication Data

Bowden, Tripp.
Freddie & me : life lessons from Freddie Bennett, Augusta National's
legendary caddie master / Tripp Bowden.
p. cm.
ISBN 978-1-60239-682-1
1. Bowden, Tripp. 2. Golfers--United States--Biography. 3. Bennett,
Freddie. 4. Caddies--United States--Biography. 5. African-American
golfers--United States--Biography. 6. Augusta National Golf
Club--History. I. Title. II. Title: Freddie and me.
GV964.B64A3 2009
796.3520922--dc22
[B]
2009001544

Printed in the United States of America

For Fletch, who never stopped believing.

CONTENTS

Prologue: Phoning Home. xiii

Part I: The Shaping of a Life

1: The Handshake 2
2: The Invitation 5
3: Night Crawlers and the Vardon Grip 8
4: My First Golf Lesson 12
5: Laughing at Humble Pie. 15
6: Christmas in July. 17
7: Magic from the Bobby Jones Sundial. 20
8: My First Golf Lesson with a Pro. 23
9: Breaking 50 with a Sledgehammer. 28
10: Big Shoes to Fill. 31
11: A Lesson in Spinning. 33
12: The First of Many Freddie-isms. 35
13: Pompano and Circumstance. 37
14: Returning the Favor. 40

Part II: Coming of Age at Augusta National

15: The Offering. 44
16: Backstage Pass. 48
17: Learning from a 1-Iron. 52
18: Perfect Practice. 54
19: Even Par, 72. 57

20: Hundred-Dollar Handshakes. 59
21: Fifteen Will Get You Twenty. 63
22: Homecoming. 65
23: Most Improved. 67
24: A Game of Catch. 69
25: How to Pay the Fiddler. 72

Part III: Higher Education

26: Open for Business. 76
27: Encyclopedia Bennett. 81
28: Dem Bones. 86
29: Fountain of Knowledge. 88
30: Eighteen Lessons. 90
31: Tuition Time. 97
32: First Steps. 100
33: Pay Out. 104
34: Caddy Logic. 106
35: Guess Who's Coming to Dinner. 108
36: Dan Quayle and Mother Theresa. 110
37: Closing Week. 113
38: The Twiddling of Thumbs. 115
39: You Can Call Me Ray. 117
40: English Humour. 119
41: The Smoking Section. 122
42: Movers and Shakers. 125
43: I'm in the Jailhouse Now. 129
44: Bric-a-Brac. 132
45: Breakfast at Tiffany's. 135
46: Same Old Lang Syne. 137
47: The Bank of Freddie. 139
48: Me and the MVP. 141
49: Benedict Arnold. 143
50: A Summer of Change. 145
51: Cuthbert. 146
52: Lightening the Mood. 149
53: Reality Bites (But Not That Hard). 151

CONTENTS

54: Chairman of the Board. 154
55: The Offer. 158
56: The Gorilla Comes Back. 163
57: Welcome Back, Kotter. 166
58: One More from the Road. 167
59: More Freddie-isms. 169
60: Promises Kept. 171
61: Second Chance of a Lifetime. 175
62: Off You Go. 177
63: Start Spreading the News. 178
64: Life in the Big City. 180
65: You Can and You Will. 183
66: Exodus. 185
67: Styrofoam Cups. 188
68: Empty Window. 191
69: Darkness Falls Today. 195
70: The Only Way I Know How. 198
71: Look Homeward, Angel. 199
72: Counting to Five. 201

Acknowledgments. 203

PROLOGUE

PHONING HOME

I'm standing over fresh dirt and stale flowers, choked up but not teary. Freddie wouldn't want teary. I fish the golf ball out of my pocket, uncap the purple Sharpie and write with an unsteady hand.

The world has lost its greatest storyteller.

I blow on the ink and drop the ball into the dirt, pushing down with my shoe so it won't roll away. It's a Titleist Pro V1, fresh out of the box. I wish it were a Top-Flite XL, a range ball in disguise. Freddie always said, "It ain't the ball, man, it's the player."

He was right.

I'm feeling terrible regret. Regret for not visiting more often after Freddie's retirement from the Augusta National Golf Club at age seventy, regret for not attending his funeral, held at Paine College's Memorial Chapel because of the expected attendance.

Turns out the church wasn't big enough, and when Pop told me the news I couldn't help but smile.

I look up, admiring the vast arrangement of flowers and cards, stuffed animals and notes. An abundant display of admiration. My eyes stop on an extravagant arrangement of chrysanthemums, roses, and lilies. *Beloved wife and mother*, the card says.

Beloved wife and mother?

Son of a bitch. I'm at the wrong grave.

I look beyond the dedication to another grave surrounded by the same goodbyes. I can't help but laugh, and I know Freddie's laughing, too. Me getting all choked up at the wrong gravesite. Even in death Freddie is alive, still looking over my shoulder and pointing me in the right direction.

I dig the Titleist out of the wet ground and walk over to his grave, still not believing he's gone.

People like Freddie aren't meant to die.

Suddenly, I am ten years old, and the ominous figure of a man with black skin and a white golf shirt is knocking on our back door.

"Hey, man. It's Freddie. Is my doctor home?"

His voice is warm as a favorite blanket, and when I open the door he shakes my hand. Just reaches out and grabs it.

It is the first handshake I remember.

I've never met Freddie before, but I recognize him from the picture in our den. He and my Pop, standing outside the bag room at Augusta. Pop smiling like he won the lottery, having just played the National for the very first time.

Another memory taps on my shoulder as I toe the dirt with my shoe. Our phone book, and the number my mom taped to the cover every year without fail. Peel it off and stick. Peel it off and stick. Freddie's private number at Augusta, the number you dialed when it was important and the only person who could make it right was Freddie. The phone was an old rotary, big and bulky. He called it the Black Bat. When it rang, Freddie stopped everything and answered it.

I push the Titleist into the dirt, close my eyes and dial the number.

It rings.

PART I
THE SHAPING OF A LIFE

1

THE HANDSHAKE

It's the summer of my tenth year of life, and I'm sitting at the kitchen table in my parents' new house, spooning chili into my mouth and staring out a bay window with yellow curtains. My mom is a great cook, Southern as a bowl of turnips. Whatever she cooks, I eat.

Some folks were raised on radio. I was raised on fatback.

Outside, the summer sun is setting on another day of me doing virtually nothing. Not that it had been too hot to play outside. When you're a ten-year-old kid, it's never too hot to play outside. But when you're a ten-year-old kid who has just been uprooted from his friends and moved across town to a busy street with speeding cars and strangers for neighbors, you don't want to go out even if it's snowing.

You don't want to do anything.

I finish my chili and fix another bowl. I sit down, and as I slide some crackers onto my plate I hear a knock at the door. I peek out the window and my eyes fall on an unfamiliar blue station wagon. It's a Buick; I know because my grandfather swears by them.

This one has seen a lot of miles.

There's another knock, gentle raps that seem thought out, and I hurry over and open the screen door.

"Hey, man, it's Freddie. My doctor home?" He says the words as if I know who he is, as if I've known him all my life.

I can't help but stare. This Freddie is a mammoth of a man, with Popeye forearms sticking out of the biggest shirt I've ever seen. The white polo is in strong contrast with Freddie's black skin, as is the scruffy mustache with a face as smooth as an apple.

My eyes lock on the shirt. On the breast is an embroidered logo of the United States, a yellow flag sticking out of Georgia. Beneath this logo are two words that will one day change my life: *Caddy Master*. But I am so far removed from the game of golf I don't come close to connecting the logo or the man to the most famous golf course in the world. In fact, the only thing I know about golf is that it takes my dad away from me.

"Hey, man, can I come in? It's hot as Marilyn Monroe out here. Had to ride with my head hanging out the window on the way over. Tongue wagging like a German shepherd puppy!"

I've never heard anybody talk like this, and I'm laughing as I let Freddie in, backing up because I can't take my eyes off him. He takes the steps two at a time, and when we're standing face-to-face, I have to crane my neck. He's six feet two if he's an inch, and even wearing soccer shoes I'm a sub sandwich from five feet.

Man, is Freddie big. Shoulders broad as a doorway.

"You must be Tripp," he says. "Doc's told me all about you."

My eyes widen. What is there to know about *me*? And how does he know my name? It takes a moment before I realize Freddie has offered his hand and I reach for it, clumsy and awkward. Freddie's big hand swallows mine, but his handshake is warm and welcoming.

"Hey, Freddie. What's shakin', man?" My father's voice is behind us, booming and baritone. He walks over and pats Freddie on the shoulder. "Looking good, man. Must be all that clean living."

"That's why I'm here, Doc. For you to tell me I feel as good as I look." He pats his heart. "Bring on the machine."

My eyes widen. The *machine*?

My dad smiles and tells Freddie to step into his office, which for this special patient means a bar stool in our den, a bowl of Planters peanuts, and a finger or two of Cutty Sark Scotch.

Pop motions for me to join them and I freeze. This has never happened before. A chance to be part of an adult conversation? With my *dad*? And this Freddie? I look behind me, thinking surely Pop must be talking to someone else.

"Come on, Tripper," he says, winking at the man who has just made an impression on me like a branding iron. "Freddie's got something he wants to tell you."

"I do?" says Freddie, winking back.

"You do," says Pop, pushing me along.

2

THE INVITATION

The den in my parents' house is a veritable golf museum. Autographed paintings of Nicklaus, Hogan, and Palmer grace the mantel above the fireplace; a driver belonging to the great Babe Zaharias hangs from brass hooks just below. Hats from golf courses all over the world—St. Andrews, Ballybunion, Lahinch, Pine Valley—all neatly aligned on cherrywood bookshelves. Above the staircase is an Augusta National beach towel, neatly pinned with Masters tickets. The oldest ticket is dated 1963, the year Nicklaus won for the very first time.

Sitting on a bar stool in our den, with a glass of scotch in one hand and peanuts in the other, is what I soon learn is a walking museum, a man with more knowledge of Augusta National Golf Club than the two men who founded it. But for now Augusta National is not what matters, at least not to Freddie. No, for now what matters most to Freddie is the most unlikely of characters.

Me.

"All right, Doc," says Freddie. "Shoot it to me straight. I'm dying, ain't I?"

"Yes and no," says my dad, deflating the blood pressure brace. It makes a crinkly crumbling sound, as if it had been holding on for dear life, wrapped tight as a tick around Freddie's massive biceps. "You're dying, but no time soon. Your ticker is strong as a horse."

Pop eases the cuff from Freddie's arm, rolls it up, and flops it on the bar.

"So I can have another one of these?" He finishes the last splash of Cutty and raises his glass. Pop twists the cap off the bottle and pours another finger.

"Doctor's orders," he says.

"This is my kind of doctor," says Freddie, his eyes on me with a smile as welcoming as a red carpet. He puts down his glass and swirls the brown liquid.

"Hey, man," he says, turning to face me. "Your daddy says you like to fish."

"I *love* to fish," I say, and it's the truth. I have dreams of becoming the next Roland Martin, disco shades and all.

"What'cha doing tomorrow?"

The question comes out of nowhere. Not because it's not a legitimate one. I'm just not expecting anyone to ask that. At least not ask that of me.

"Nothing," I say.

"That settles it then," says Freddie, popping a handful of peanuts into his mouth. "Me and you are gonna catch us a couple hundred bream tomorrow. I'll pick you up in the morning. Eight o'clock all right?"

"Sure," I say, so excited my prepubescent voice reaches the pitch of a dog whistle.

"I've got my own stuff," I say. "Got a brand new rod and reel for Christmas. A Zebco 460 with a graphite rod. Almost caught an alligator snapping turtle with it, but he bit the line before I could reel him in."

"Better be glad he did," says Freddie, smiling. "'Cause you woulda been next. Those sonofabitches are mean as a scorned woman."

I don't know a lot about women, much less a scorned one, but it doesn't matter. I'm hanging on Freddie's every word. It feels pretty special to have an adult that wants to talk with me.

"That's some high-end stuff you got there," says Freddie. "But you won't need any of that where we're going. It'll only slow you down."

"Slow me down?"

"Yeah, man. You ain't *never* seen fishing like this. We'll catch 'em so fast you'll be huffing and puffing like the Big Bad Wolf."

I'm laughing now, a smile on my face big as the moon. "I can't wait."

"Me neither," says Freddie, pulling his keys out of his pocket. But he's not quite ready to go.

"So where you taking him?" asks my dad.

"The club," says Freddie. "Best fishing in the world."

The expression on my face says I should know what the "club" is, but I don't.

"He means the Augusta National Golf Club," says Pop, beaming.

That should mean something to me, but it doesn't.

My life was about to change forever, but I didn't know that either.

3

NIGHT CRAWLERS AND THE VARDON GRIP

I'm riding down Berckmans Road in Freddie's old station wagon, my legs sticking to the vinyl seat and a warm summer wind whipping my hair. Freddie is manning the wheel, his huge hands leaving no doubt as to who is in control. At the moment, we're silent, but the silence suits just fine. Freddie has a special gift for making folks feel at home no matter where they are, and though this is just the second time I've seen the man, I feel like I've known him all my life. We stop at the light and he turns to me.

"Worms or crickets?"

"Huh?" I say, still staring out the window, not believing I am here, on a fishing trip with someone who isn't a parent or an uncle. Freddie told me not to call him sir.

I ain't no sir. I'm Freddie. Just like you're Tripp.

"Worms or crickets?" he asks. "Which ones you like fishing with the most?"

It is the first time an adult has ever asked for my opinion.

"Worms," I say, turning to face him, my voice surprisingly strong and confident. I have no idea where this new strength is coming from.

"Red wigglers or night crawlers?"

Uh-oh, multiple choice. I hate multiple choice. Whenever I don't have the chance to bullshit, I'm in trouble. Even at the age of ten.

Freddie senses my hesitation. "Ain't no right or wrong answers in fishing, man."

I smile. "In that case, I say night crawlers."

Freddie reaches under his seat, pulls out a Cool Whip tub and hands it over. I don't have to open it to know what's inside.

"Fishing's all about the opposites," says Freddie. "Night crawlers in the day. Red wigglers at night. Cane poles; forget rod and reels. And unless you're trying to catch Moby Dick, it's banks not boats. Crickets anytime, unless there's no moon. Doesn't take much light to bounce off a cricket, especially when he's dangling from a cork."

Freddie flicks on the blinker. "Yellow or red?"

Bouncing light? Yellow or red? I have no idea what Freddie is talking about but it doesn't matter. It's all I can do not to pinch myself and make sure I'm not dreaming. Except for my parents and an uncle who scares me shitless, no adult has ever taken me anywhere.

I don't pinch myself for the dreaming, for fear that I just might be.

"Yellow," I say.

"Good guess," says Freddie, packing out a Marlboro Red that he lights in a single motion, smooth as a Velvet Elvis. "But ain't nothing wrong with guessing. Lot better to guess than just sit there with your thumb in your mouth."

I'm laughing as Freddie takes a right on Washington Road, still laughing as he pulls into Augusta National and heads down Magnolia Lane with just a raised finger and a "Hey, man" to the gun-toting guard at the gate. The guard is tall as a cornstalk, three hundred pounds if he's an ounce. He waves back as if he just won the election.

Although I was born and raised in Augusta, I am too young and too removed from the game of golf to realize what Augusta National really is, what it means to our town, the world, and the game; the history, nostalgia, prestige, and secrecy. Though I will one day earn a Division I golf scholarship and even make it to the final stage of a British Open qualifier, all I know about golf at this point is that it's a stupid sport that takes up too much of my father's time and I would rather kick a soccer ball into a net, or stay home and read a book.

Truth be told, at this point in my life I hate the game of golf.

But I *love* to fish.

Freddie parks the station wagon in the members' lot, hops out and pops open the trunk. He pulls out four bamboo cane poles and a cooler filled with ice. He tells me he'll be right back and he is, with a no-topper golf cart. We load up all the goods, and when Freddie sees I'm safely in, he guns the cart toward the Par 3 course. It's an E-Z-GO with the governor removed, and I'm amazed by how fast it goes.

"Ike's Pond is good for fishing, but only when the bream are on bed," says Freddie as we hightail it down the path. "But that ain't 'til late summer. We're gonna fish the Big Pond today."

I nod, game for anything. Big Pond, Ike's Pond. It's all the same to me.

Freddie cuts through a corner row of bushes, eases off the gas, and coasts down a hill of grass so green it doesn't seem real. We're silent again, and all I can see is the surreal visual of green and more green and the sun bouncing off water as calm as the Pope. Freddie pulls up on the bank, locks the brake and grabs the cane poles and cooler. I bring the night crawlers.

Freddie opens the tub of worms and quickly baits all four hooks. "Next one you bait yourself," he says.

I nod.

He winks. "The fish here are big, so hold on with both hands."

I'm thinking Jonah and the whale.

As soon as the first pole drops into the water, Freddie pulls in a bream the size of my head. He pulls out the hook, worm still intact and tosses the fish onto the bank. "No time for stringers. Plus, the snapping turtles will eat 'em dead to rights soon as you put 'em in the water. We'll toss them in the cooler, so don't worry about that. You ready?"

I nod, knowing that after what I just witnessed I am nowhere near ready.

Freddie hands me my cane pole, a long piece of bamboo that is baited and good to go. I drop the night crawler into the water and turn to speak, and as I do the pole is almost snatched from my hand. I pull back, hands shaking on the pole as I stand up. A bream big as my shoe dangles in the air.

Holy Majoly. What kind of place *is* this?

"You know how to get him loose?"

"I do," I say, wiggling the hook out of the bream's mouth. I toss him onto the bank, then quickly walk back and throw him into the cooler. Freddie's eyes are on me.

"Part of the Big Man's plan. Long as you eat what you catch, He's all right with it. And that's all we're doing here." Freddie pulls in another bream, big as a lunch box.

This goes on for an hour or more, and when I throw the last bream into the cooler I see that the green Igloo is chock full. You couldn't catch this many fish in an aquarium!

"Doc says you don't like golf. Why's that?"

The question is from out of nowhere, though I soon learn none of Freddie's questions are from out of nowhere. Neither are his answers.

"It's a stupid game," I say, closing the lid. It's a lie but I'm telling the truth.

"Maybe, maybe not. You ever give it a chance?"

Give it a chance? I never thought of it like that.

I shake my head. Pop tried to welcome me into the game but I wouldn't let him. I'd rather play soccer or fish Rae's Creek. My old man loved golf, and I hated how it took him away from me.

"Whoa—check out this whopper!" Freddie pulls up another monster bream and throws it onto the bank, smiling as I catch it on the second bounce and toss it into the cooler.

"We need to talk," says Freddie, grabbing my fishing pole.

4

MY FIRST GOLF LESSON

"Come here," says Freddie. "I want to show you something."

I walk over to where Freddie is standing. Our reflections bounce off the water, and we look a lot like Mutt and Jeff. He hands me back my cane pole.

"All right, man. What do you know about marriage?"

"Marriage?"

"Don't worry. I ain't about to marry you off like some kid from the Gypsy Camp," he laughs. "Just making a point. I know you said earlier you didn't like golf. But you also said you never gave it a chance. I'm not going to force you to play. This ain't about that. Just want you to give it a chance. That cool?"

I shrug my shoulders, nod my head. No way could I ever say no to Freddie.

"Okay," he says. "I want you to do as I do. If I go too fast, tell me, and I'll slow down."

"Okay," I say.

"Hold that pole out in front of you, like this." Freddie angles the tip of the cane pole towards the water, about a forty five-degree angle, and the bobber dangles just above the surface. I do the same. "Now, take off all your fingers but the index, the one you use to point at all the pretty girls. Perfect. Now listen close, because this is the most important lesson in golf. If you don't master this, you'll never go any further than the windmill."

I scrunch my face. "The windmill?"

"Putt-Putt," he says.

"Gotcha," I say, smiling.

"The grip is your only connection to the club, and through the club the ball, and you better believe the ball knows when you two ain't getting along."

Freddie pauses for a moment, and I'm suddenly aware how quiet it is. Like if I listened closely enough I could hear my own heartbeat, the blood coursing through my veins.

I nod again.

"The secret, like all secrets, is simple: Grip it in the fingers, just like you would a baseball. That's where all the power hides. And if anyone ever tells you to grip the sonofabitch like a baby bird or a tube of toothpaste with the cap off, walk away—fast as you can." He laughs. "All right, now do as I do."

I mirror Freddie as he puts both hands on the fishing pole, just like he would a golf club. It's hard to tell how close I am to getting it right because my hands are half the size of his, but he nods, so I must be doing okay.

"All right, now. I want you to grip it tight enough to hold on to, but light enough to feel a nibble. No more and no less. And when you feel that fish hit, take all but your index finger off the pole, and pull that fish in fast as you can. If you're gripping it right, that index finger is all you're gonna need."

Here I am, at Augusta National Golf Club, standing on the edge of the most beautiful pond I've ever seen. Everything in perfect order, the stars aligned, the yellow bobber disappearing below the surface.

I haven't ruled out the fact I could be dreaming every single bit of this.

"Let's see it, man. Snatch that sonofabitch out the water!"

The old me would've chickened out, would have held that cane pole tight as a Catholic nun to a ruler, but the old me is gone. I quickly take my left hand off the pole, then all but the trigger finger of my right. The cane pole is locked in the crook, bouncing from the weight of the fish but secure as Buckingham Palace.

I'm not quite ready to "snatch that sonofabitch out the water," being just ninety pounds with a brick in each pocket, but I'm fully capable of walking backwards and so I do, pulling a bream as big as my shoe out of the water, using just one finger, exactly as Freddie had said. Freddie walks over, grabs the flopping fish, and pulls out the hook.

"So what'cha think, man?"

"I'm thinking nobody will ever believe me."

"Long as you believe, it doesn't matter."

I nod. He's right. It really doesn't matter.

Freddie walks over to the edge of the pond and slips the fish into the water, then wipes his hands on his pants and rubs them together. He turns to me and smiles.

"Can't keep the teacher, man."

5

LAUGHING AT HUMBLE PIE

It's another day of fishing and the bream are hopping out of Ike's Pond so fast you'd think it was on fire. The big green Igloo cooler is again almost full, and I've pulled in so many fish my shoulder aches. But when they're biting like this, it's impossible to stop.

"I think you're ready," says Freddie, laying his pole on the lush grass.

I hadn't noticed what he'd been holding in his other hand, lost as I was in the wonderful world of catching fish after fish after fish after—

"Ready?" "Ready for what?"

"Ready to hit one. Your first golf shot."

I'm really ready to land another shoe-sized bream, but no way am I saying that to Freddie.

"Sure," I say, hopping into the E-Z-GO. Freddie guns it along the edge of the Big Pond then up the hill to the tee box. I hop out like a bunny.

Except for the pond that looms in the distance, the 4th hole on Augusta's famous Par 3 course is not particularly intimidating. It's half the distance of a football field, give or take an incomplete pass. I bet I could *throw* the ball onto the green from where we're standing.

Turns out that would have been a better idea.

"All right, man," says Freddie. "Show me what you got." He hands me the wedge and points to the ball he just dropped on the tee box. "Let it ride!"

Let what ride? I've never hit a golf ball in my life.

"Use that grip I showed you. Then just take it back and bring it through. Golf ain't near as hard as folks make it out to be."

"I don't know if I can, Freddie. I've never done this before."

"Sure you have. Hundreds of times. You're one of those with that born-in swing, I bet. Just use that grip and let it ride."

I let it ride, all right.

In one of those moments that happen so fast you're not sure they happen at all, I grab the wedge, wrap my skinny fingers around the worn grip, take the club back, and bring it through as hard as I can, as fast as I can.

As bad as I can.

The clubface catches the practice ball dead center, like a karate chop to the gut, and the Titleist screams toward the green like a wingless bird, bouncing twice before diving into the pond. The edges of the ponds at Augusta slope straight down, which is good for fishing, bad for ball finding.

That one's gone.

"Man," says Freddie, his face breaking into a big smile. "That thing didn't get knee-high to a grasshopper!"

I laugh at myself until my stomach aches.

6

CHRISTMAS IN JULY

There's a knock on the door, but this time I don't hear it. I'm in the back of the house, flopped on my bed, reading the latest *Golf Digest*. I'm on page 56, trying to make sense of an instructional article that is comparing the golf swing to a pendulum, the rhythm to a metronome, the outcome to an act of Congress.

It makes about as much sense as one-legged kickball.

My mother's voice travels down the hall like a salesman on a mission. "Sugar, there's somebody here to see youuuu!"

I dog-ear the article and follow her voice into the kitchen.

"Hey, man. I got something for you." It's Freddie, an imposing figure in his triple-XL white golf shirt, black Sansabelts, and Gucci shoes. No socks.

"Hey, Freddie."

He motions me over to the kitchen table and my jaw drops like it was tied to a boat anchor.

"There you go," he says. "All yours."

Lying on the table and neatly arranged is everything a golfer could dream of except the perfect swing. A dozen Titleist balata golf balls, two leather gloves with the Augusta logo front and center, a big pack of tees, and a shag bag so full of balls it looks pregnant.

"Open it," says Freddie, pointing to the green shag bag.

I work the zipper—it glides like a waterslide—and when the bag is open I put my hand inside and dig around. I pull out a golf ball, striped green with the pros' names on the side. It's been hit once or twice and smells like rye grass.

"Official practice balls from the Masters Tournament. Best players in the world have been hitting those little darlins. Got some good mojo on 'em. Might come in handy while you're learning the game. These might come in handy, too, come to think of it."

Freddie reaches behind the pantry door and pulls out a set of golf clubs.

"Walter Hagens, man. Best match player in the game, that fella. Lots of folks play golf with their heads—Hagen played with his heart. Big difference, but I ain't gotta tell you that." He pushes the clubs toward me. "They're junior clubs, so they'll fit you just right. Matched set. Only company that makes 'em, far as I know."

"Wow," I say, lifting out a 3-iron. I rub my hand across the clubface, my fingers along the grooves. These clubs have never even been hit. There's not a mark on them.

"Fresh from the factory," says Freddie. "Hand forged. Steel blades. The real deal. A pro's club."

I nod, dumbfounded. My search for words comes up empty.

"Go on," says Freddie. "Show me that grip."

I place my hands on the tacky black grip, tap the blade on our linoleum floor.

"Looks good, man. Don't forget the waggle."

I don't.

"I think you're good to go," says Freddie. "Clubs, balls, tees, gloves."

I look around, still gripping the 3-iron. Freddie reads my mind.

"You wondering where the shoes are, ain'tcha?"

"No," I answer.

I can feel Freddie's eyes on me.

"Um, yeah. I guess I was."

"Break fifty on nine holes, and I'll get you some shoes. Show me some dedication, show me that you love the game, and I'll get you some FootJoys. Any color, any style. But I don't want to hear about your mama buying you a pair." He throws her a wink. "No shoes until you break fifty, man. Ain't no clowns out there breaking fifty, I promise you that. Break fifty and I'll know you're serious about learning the game."

"You got it," I say.

I've never been so serious about anything in my life.

My mom walks over and puts her arm on the big man's shoulder. "Freddie, this is just wonderful. What do we owe you?"

"Commitment," he says, leaving me with that all-encompassing word, smiling as he walks out the door.

7

MAGIC FROM THE
BOBBY JONES SUNDIAL

I have no way of knowing now, but I will never see Freddie swing a golf club. He'll show me his grip (it looks just like Arnold Palmer's, down to the meaty V of the right hand), his waggle (Palmer's again), even his stance, with toes pointed out like a young Jack Nicklaus.

But never the swing.

After this story I'm about to tell you, I'm not really sure it matters.

It's my very first Masters and I'm with my dad, standing outside Gate 10, waiting to show our practice round tickets to a Pinkerton guard. Augusta is years away from making practice-round tickets lottery only, and we just walked up to the ticket window and bought them.

We enter the gate and my dad makes a beeline for the food tent, where we buy BBQ sandwiches on squishy white bread for fifty cents and Cokes for a quarter each. We eat as we walk and as we crest the hill my eyes fall on an endless sea of patrons. Thousands of people, from every walk of life. I'm amazed how quiet it is. I can actually hear the grass under my feet flattening as I walk. If someone dropped a pin, I bet it would echo like a yodel.

My dad takes a sip of Coke, washes down the last bite of his sandwich, and points. "Check this out, Tripper."

I'm looking, not real sure what to make of it. I can tell it's a sundial, but I don't recognize or know the significance of a certain man's likeness on top.

"That's Bobby Jones," says Pop. "He and a gentleman named Clifford Roberts founded this place and started the Masters. Back in the thirties, when all the world was young."

I touch the sundial. These are the days of minimum security, and the only yellow ropes you see are on the golf course. The only way you know that the area beyond the sundial—the pro shop and bag room—is off limits is the presence of a Pinkerton guard, sweating like a blacksmith in his thick, navy blue uniform.

"What time is it?"

I look down at the sundial. "Twelve o'clock. High noon."

Pop shakes his head.

"It's time to tell you why this sundial is so famous. And it's not because one of the greatest golfers in the history of the game is standing on top of it. No, sir. It's because of that man in there." He points to the left side of the pro shop.

Freddie's office.

"Let me set the stage for you," says Pop, pointing down the hill directly opposite the sundial. "See that green down there? Waaay down there. The one over the service road."

"I see it," I say.

"That's hole number two, for those taking notes. How far would you say that is?"

I take a stab. "Four hundred yards."

"Not bad. But more like four eighty-five, give or take a step." Pop sets down his Coke and takes a stance, pretending he's gripping a driver. He doesn't look up.

"Imagine I'm holding an old Tony Penna driver. Head scratched up like a tomcat, grip slick as a salesman. I tee up a Titleist that's just as old, waggle a few times, then let her rip. No practice swing, no stretching. I just got up from my desk, walked out the door, and let it ride, Clyde."

I stare at my dad, not sure where this is going.

He looks up at me, hands still gripping the pretend golf club.

"Oh, forgot to mention one other minor detail."

"What's that?"

"Guess what kind of shoes I'm wearing?"

"FootJoy," I say, wishing I had a pair.

"Bedroom slippers," says Pop.

"Bedroom slippers?"

Pop draws back the pretend club and follows through, posing on the imaginary shot as if it were the best drive of his life. Considering it bounced onto the 2nd green and almost went in the hole, I guess it would have been.

"Freddie drove—wait—Freddie drove the 2nd green from up here? Wearing bedroom slippers?"

Pop nods. "And not so much as a single practice swing. Said it was the first shot he'd hit in five years. Damnedest thing I've ever seen. Come on," he says, patting my shoulder. "Let's go see the man behind the myth. See if he's still got that magic driver."

Pop waves to the security guard, tells him we're here to see Freddie, and we walk into the forbidden land that is behind-the-scenes Augusta National, just like we were members. Turns out we're one better.

We are friends with Freddie.

8

MY FIRST GOLF LESSON
WITH A PRO

My first official golf lesson takes place in the most unlikely of places on the most unusual of days: the Augusta National Golf Club, the Monday after the Masters.

Talk about your intimidating stages.

I'm riding down Magnolia Lane in my mother's car, brand-new glove on one hand and faded tennis shoes on my feet. Freddie greets us in the members' parking lot, which is packed with cars and people. Milling about and scrambling for tee times are the chosen ones, lucky stiffs who've been granted a once-in-a-lifetime chance to play the most exclusive golf course in the world the day after the conclusion of golf's most coveted major. The tees, the pins, even the scoreboards are all exactly as they were only twenty-four hours ago, when a young Tom Watson shot 67 to clip the great Jack Nicklaus by two.

Much of this is lost on me, however, as I know little of Tom Watson and even less of Nicklaus.

But I do know Jerry Pate, the defending U.S. Open Champion. Just three days ago I watched him hit practice balls in a driving rain, orange Prostaffs soaring into a gunmetal sky, his caddy holding an umbrella over the champion's head after each swing was finished.

I know because I'm standing in the exact same spot.

"Hey, pahds. I'm Mike Shannon. What's the good word?"

He offers a hand and we shake.

"Hi," I say.

"Mike, this is Tripp Bowden. My doctor's son," says Freddie, smiling. "The kid I told you about. Think you can work a little magic on him?"

Magic?

"Shoooot, yeah. He even looks like a player."

I do?

"All right, then. I'll leave you two to have at it." Freddie turns to face me. "Listen to him, man. He might not look like it, but this cat knows his stuff."

My mom is clutching her pocketbook, jangling her keys.

"Any chance I could do a little shopping, Freddie? I need to buy a couple shirts and time just got away from me yesterday. We got so caught up in the excitement we never made it past sixteen."

"Got caught up in the beer tent, too, I bet," says Freddie, in a voice only I can hear, before turning to my mother. "Absolutely, Mrs. Bowden. Shop till you drop. Tell them I said give you the Charleston discount, okay?"

"You're a dear, Freddie Bennett," says Mom as she hurries into the pro shop.

"All right, pahds. You ready?"

I follow the voice. This Mike guy is young, twenty-five I'm guessing, but he looks like a little kid, not much bigger than me. *He's* gonna teach me golf?

My worries are soon over when Mike launches the first of five towering drives into a big green net at the end of the range. I have no idea how far he's hitting it, but as I look around at the other golfers, no one is coming close. Some have even stopped what they were doing, unable to take their eyes off Mike.

"Freddie says you're the pro here," I say. What I really want to say is, Wow—you can sure knock the shit out of a golf ball!

"*Assistant* pro," says Mike. "Maybe one day I'll run with the big dogs." He props his driver, a big Tony Penna with a blond finish, against my golf bag and looks inside.

"Say, look at what you've got. Real blades. Where'd you get these babies?"

Mike pulls out my 7-iron, grips it, and sends a ball sailing into the distance. The club is a little short for him, but not by much.

"Who cut these down for you? Freddie?"

I shake my head. "They came that way. But yeah, Freddie gave them to me."

"Nice," says Mike. "Birthday gift or something?"

"Just something, I guess. Freddie showed up at the house one day and handed them over. Shag bag and balls and gloves too." I hold up my left hand, show him the brand-new glove with the Augusta National logo embroidered on the strap.

"Look at you," he says. "All logo-ed up like a member." He points to my glove and then my shirt, a pink polo with the Augusta logo in full view. "All you're missing is a Green Jacket!"

I stop laughing when he looks down at my shoes.

"No spikes, eh?"

"Freddie said I had to break fifty before he would get me some. Said he didn't want to hear about my mama buying me a pair or he'd make her take 'em back."

Mike laughs.

"That Freddie's a piece of work, no doubt. But he's a great guy. Good man to have on your team." Mike grips the 7-iron, brushing the grass as he talks. "Freddie tells me you and him do a lot of fishing out here. Down by the Par 3. Says you catch 'em hand over fist."

"I've never seen fish like that in my life," I say.

"Yeah, this place is something, all right. Got the best of everything—even the fishing. Who would think some of the best fishing in the world is at Augusta National?"

Mike hands me the 7-iron. I put it back in the bag.

"No, pahds. I want to see what you got. Freddie said he taught you a few things. Says you got a pretty mean grip. Let's see it."

I pull out the 7-iron, wrap my hands around the tacky rubber handle.

"Whoa, check you out. You look like Ben Hogan holding that thing. Shoot, man. You don't need any of *my* help." He laughs and tosses a ball at my feet. "Freddie teach you that grip?"

I nod. "With a fishing pole."

"A fishing pole?"

"Yep."

"Ain't that something? But with Freddie Bennett, nothing surprises me. Not anymore."

Mike bends down and tees up a Titleist. "All right, pahds. Let's see what you got."

Uh-oh. The last time somebody said that to me the ball went nose-diving into a pond.

I look away. The practice tee at Augusta National is a sea of green. Thick, lush grass as far as the eye can see. Not a drop of water in sight.

I rare back and swing as hard as I can. The ball dribbles off the tee.

Mike quickly bends down and pegs up another, though it's clear he could just take two steps, pick up my shot, and place it back on the tee.

Another fierce swing and another dribbler. Who said tees make things easier?

This goes on for what seems like forever, though in reality only a minute or two, because there are only a few balls at my feet, barely outside the cast of my shadow.

"I see your problem," says Mike. "You're standing too close to the ball."

I look down. Something drips on my shoes. Sweat? Tears?

"I'm standing too close to the ball?"

Mike puts a hand on my shoulder, points to the grouping of balls not six feet away.

"Yeah, pahds. *After* you hit it." He laughs and so do I.

How can I not?

"Don't sweat it, pahds. Golf is a bitch to learn, but it's a beautiful game and you can play it for the rest of your life. You've only been playing for five minutes, man. Don't worry—we'll get you straightened out. This is the Augusta National. Magic happens out here."

I'm thinking it's gonna take a lot more than magic to straighten me out. Breaking 50 suddenly seems a thousand miles away.

"Let's start with your stance," says Mike, positioning my feet shoulder width apart. "And let's bend a little more from the waist, like a basketball player getting ready to guard somebody. Relax those shoulders a little. That's a 7-iron you've got in your hands, not a machete. You're not trying to kill anything with it." Mike tees up another, looks at me, and smiles.

"Now forget everything I just told you and launch that sucker."

I wind up and give my 7-iron a rip, clipping the ball off the tee as neat as you please. It flies like a bell curve onto a green some hundred yards out.

When the ball bounces twice and spins to a stop, I almost fall down.

"Whoa!" I say.

Mike is really smiling now.

"Say, pahds. You ever hear of a guy named Harvey Penick?"

9

BREAKING 50 WITH A SLEDGEHAMMER

If there is a game harder than golf, I've not played it. To complicate matters, the USGA rule book is one big riddle, and the book of decisions is thicker than a New York phone book.

There are few things worse than being an eleven-year-old beginner golfer, armed only with a set of forged blades and tennis shoes, a face covered in sunscreen, and a few fundamentals bowling around in your head. A gutter ball here, a gutter ball there.

I'm still waiting for my first strike, and with the sun sinking behind the trees like a slippery lemon, I'm pretty sure it won't happen today.

I look at my watch. A summer's day in the South is longer than a Rockette's legs, and even though it's 7:30, there's still time to squeeze in nine holes, even for a scrub like me.

Play fast, man. Hit it and get it. Play fast, and people won't care how bad you are. Not saying you're bad. You're just a beginner. Hell, even Shakespeare was a beginner.

I suppose Freddie's right, about playing fast, I mean. Still, I'm having as much trouble finding playing partners as a fat kid at recess. No one, and I mean no one, wants to play with an eleven-year-old beginner golfer.

With the exception of the few rounds I've played with Pop, all my trips around the track have been solo flights. I'm the pilot, copilot, flight attendant, and passenger. But at least I'm quick about it. To hell with breaking 50 for a pair of FootJoys. My best nine to date is a 62.

At least until today.

After a mix of bogeys, double bogeys, and a lone par on the 5th, I'm standing on the 7th tee ten over par. If I bogey out I shoot 49, and the FootJoys are mine.

The 7th hole at West Lake Country Club is a straightforward par 4 with a downhill green guarded by a gnarly pine and a bunker shaped like Mickey Mouse ears. After a solid drive that almost crests the hill, I stripe a 5-wood that takes a bad kick and dives into Mickey's left ear like a kite with no tail. But the lie is a good one, with the ball sitting up and plenty of green between me and the flag. I could blast it out and two-putt. Heck, maybe even one-putt.

Par is still a possibility.

I pull out my wedge (no sand wedge yet, but I've asked for one for Christmas), size up my bunker shot, and quickly conclude that they don't get much easier than this. My Titleist couldn't be sitting any prettier if it was on a tee.

I choke down on the grip, dig my tennis shoes into the sand. For every inch I dig in, I grip another inch down. Just like Freddie told me. Settled in, I aim my shoulders, hips, legs, and feet left of the target, keeping the clubface open. A couple of waggles, and I'm ready to go.

Except I'm not.

On my second waggle the clubface dusts the sand, just barely, but enough for me to feel it. There had been a hard rain the night before, and the sand is packed down like clay. I didn't see it, but I sure felt it.

This is not good. Here's why—USGA Rule 13-4: Before making a stroke at a ball that is in a hazard (bunker or water), the player must not touch the ground in the hazard with his hand or club. Penalty for breach of rule. Match play—loss of hole; stroke play—two strokes.

A two-stroke penalty. Damn. There goes any hope of breaking 50. Wait, you say. You're by yourself. Playing alone. No one will ever know.

Yeah, but *I'll* know.

I step out of the bunker, collect myself best I can, step back in the bunker, and settle in. The shot is a damn good one, and the Titleist takes two big hops before skidding to a stop six inches from the cup.

It's the best bunker shot I've ever hit!

I tap in the gimme, pull a sweaty scorecard from my pocket, and write down my score.

Six.

If I hadn't grazed the sand, a rules infraction no one witnessed but me, I would've had a four. Freddie's voice is in my head: *If a frog had pockets, he'd carry guns and shoot snakes.*

This frog may not have pockets, but he's honest as the day is long, and I know he'll sleep just fine tonight.

A double bogey never felt so good.

10

BIG SHOES TO FILL

It's August one year later, and I'm standing on the 9th green of a little afterthought of a golf course called Randolph Country Club. Don't let the name fool you. The only thing country about this place is its location.

My clubs are on the edge of the tiny green, the matching set of Walter Hagens that Freddie surprised me with. They're forged blades, with a clubface as small as the ball. Freddie's voice is in my ear. *Learn to hit these babies and you can write your ticket. Ain't no tour pro ever cut his teeth on a set of cavity backs, I can promise you that.*

I believe him. These clubs are harder to hit than a Nolan Ryan fastball.

My first set of clubs, first sleeve of Titleists, first glove, and first pack of tees were all gifts from Freddie. After the grip lesson there were only a few others, Freddie saying he was more qualified to give life lessons than golf lessons. He made me promise to find a pro I trusted, and stick with him.

I did.

His name is Tom Moore.

But I can't get Freddie's lessons out of my head as I stand over this four-footer to break 50 for the very first time. I look down at my feet and hear Freddie's voice.

Break fifty, man, and the FootJoys are yours. But not until you do. You break fifty and I'll know you're serious about learning the game.

I'm so serious my hands are shaking. The four-footer looks forty; the hole is now a thimble, the ball a marble. I'd close my eyes if I thought it would help.

It doesn't.

Again, Freddie's voice is in my ear: *Putting is all about feel, man. Feel and going with your gut. Just like life. Make the decision you believe in and give it a chance to happen. Don't look; listen. Let the ball tell you whether you were right or wrong.*

I draw back my Bulls Eye putter and wait for the answer.

11

A LESSON IN SPINNING

It's a Friday night, the summer of my thirteenth year. Most of my friends are out roaming the streets, smoking Swisher Sweets and drinking liquor from their old man's stash, telling stories about girls and wishing they were true.

They can have it.

Me, I'm sitting on a barstool in the family den, an eight-ounce bottled Coke burning my throat as I wash down my second bowl of peanuts. They're Spanish nuts with the skin on—Freddie's favorite. And of course, my favorite too.

Freddie is telling Pop about some of the latest changes at Augusta—adding some trees to the rough between 15 and 17. By trees he means thirty-footers, not some seedlings you pick up at the local nursery.

"Big as the ones out there," he says, pointing to the sea of towering loblolly pines that canvases our backyard.

Pop shakes his head. "When money is no object."

"You got that right," says Freddie, swirling his glass. "Okay, Doc. I got a good one for you."

"Lay it on me."

Freddie's eyes are on mine.

"I can leave," I say.

Pop shakes his head. "*You* can stay. You're thirteen. I think you can handle it." Pop smiles and I grin like a circus clown.

I lean in as if expecting Freddie to whisper, to tell the story so softly my mother can't hear him. Not that she would care. I have no way of knowing this at thirteen, but my mom loves off-color jokes.

Freddie begins.

"Two buddies are walking through the forest, gonna do a little coon hunting. Got the dogs howling, a moonlit sky, shotguns at the ready. They don't get too far before one old boy says, 'Man, I gotta bust me a piss something fierce.' So he props his shotgun against a tree and commences to getting down to business. He's about to shake the dew off his lily when *SNAP!* A rattlesnake springs up and bites him right on his joint.

"The old boy drops to his knees, screaming to beat the band. His buddy runs over, sees the rattlesnake slither away, sees his best friend clutching his joint like a rope and it's the only thing keeping him from falling off a cliff. His buddy looks down and says, 'Hang tight, man, hang tight. I'm gonna run and get the Doc. You gonna be Okay. You gonna make it—just hang tight!'

"His buddy hightails it through the woods to the ol' country doctor, bangs on the door and tells him what happened. Doc says not to worry, says he wishes he could go and treat the injury personally, but he's gotta make a house call on the Widder Johnson. Doc tells him, 'Now all you gotta do is make a small incision in the snake bite and then suck out the venom, fast as you can.' Then he hands the buddy a scalpel and sends him on his way.

"So the old boy runs back and sees his friend still on the ground, pants around his ankles, just a writhing in pain. The friend rolls over, his voice all weak, and whispers, 'What'd the Doc say?'

"The old boy looks at his buddy, his buddy's unit, and then his buddy in the eye.

"'Doc says you gonna die.'"

I laugh so hard I wonder if I'll ever stop.

12

THE FIRST OF MANY FREDDIE-ISMS

"If you can't putt, you can't play," says Freddie. "It's as simple as that."

I have no way of knowing it, but this will be the last golf lesson Freddie ever gives me.

"You know what I mean by that?"

I shake my head. I have an idea, but I'd rather hear it from Freddie. I just love hearing the man talk.

"Golf is all about getting the ball in the hole. That's the bottom line. Driver won't do it. Irons won't do it. Wishing, hoping, and praying won't do it. The flat-stick is the most important club in your bag. If you ever want to be a player and not just a golfer, you need to learn how to use that little lady as if your life depended on it."

"If you can't putt, you can't play," I say to myself. I'm still not exactly sure what Freddie means, and it's apparently written all over my face, because he continues his explanation.

"Think of your putter as Jesus. She'll forgive all your sins if you put your faith and trust in her. There ain't no pictures on the scorecard. A four is a four, whether you boomed a drive, staked your approach, and two-putted—or hooked your tee shot, punched out, knocked a wedge on the green, and holed a fifty-footer. The flat-stick is the great equalizer. It doesn't care how big you are, how strong you are. But it's *high* on familiarity." He points to my 8813 Wilson putter, a "gift" from a talented instructor named Mike Hebron, a gift my mom arranged after a visit to Mike's club on Long Island. I'm not entirely sure it was a gift, but its arrival was not surprising. My mom could make the Pope surrender his miter.

I pull the nickel blade from my bag and grip it, both thumbs flat and fingers relaxed.

"You probably won't be the longest guy out there, may not be the best striker of the ball, but there ain't no, and I mean *no*, reason you can't be the best putter out there."

Me? The best putter in golf?

"I'll leave you two alone," he says, patting me on the shoulder. "I bet y'all got some catching up to do."

Thirty years later, that putter is still in my bag.

13

POMPANO AND CIRCUMSTANCE

My first attempt to make my eighth-grade junior high golf team ends badly, and though I'm discouraged by the nine-hole total of 54, I am encouraged by the consistency. Nine straight double bogeys. No birdies, no pars—not even the random snowman. Just doubles out the wazoo.

I try to find the good in the bad as surely there must be, so I spend every waking moment away from school on the golf course. Over time my game steadily improves, in spite of my lack of born-with-it talent, and bogeys and pars soon replace doubles. On rare occasions, a birdie flies its way onto my scorecard.

My ninth-grade year at Tutt Junior High could not be any better. I'm dating a cheerleader who happens to be the sweetest, most beautiful girl I've ever known, the sun is always shining, and, as of 3:45 P.M. on a Thank God It's Friday, I'm standing on the 1st tee of the Augusta Golf Course, a local muni affectionately known as the Cabbage Patch, eager to show the golf coach I'm ready for my letterman's jacket.

I just lied.

About the first part.

My girlfriend and I broke up last night over something stupid, something I said and now regret so badly it's all I can do to tie my shoes, much less swing a golf club. As I stand on the 1st tee, desperately trying to focus on the matter at hand, it becomes painfully obvious there is no way in hell my ball is going to find the fairway.

It doesn't.

A lackluster swing with a driver that feels like a fairground sledgehammer sends my Titleist barrel-rolling down the left side of the severely sloped terrain, and the sickening sound of ball on concrete road, a road that also doubles as out-of-bounds, puts a bowling ball in my stomach. When my second drive mirrors the first, it's all I can do not to puke on my FootJoys.

I want to go home and I want to go now.

But I don't, and nine holes later I hand my scorecard to our coach, a physics teacher who surprisingly plays a pretty mean stick. She was only holding team tryouts because school board requirements demanded as much. In her mind, the team was already formed and I was going to be one of the lucky five.

Not anymore. Not with a 49 staring me down like a vulture.

Coach stares at my scorecard, puts her eyes on mine. "What in God's name happened to you, Bowden? You break a bone or something?"

"Fletch broke up with me. Last night, on the phone. Not her fault. I mean—aw, Coach. I'm a basket case."

Coach wrinkles her nose and does something I will never forget.

She crumples up my scorecard.

"I strongly suggest you get those eggs back in the basket, Bowden. There is going to be a *second* nine-hole qualifier, just to make sure the top-five finishers from today are truly top-five caliber. Do you get me?"

My mouth drops open. "Really?"

Coach hands me my crumpled scorecard.

"Same time, same place, same Bat channel. You have one week to get your life in order, Bowden. I suggest you get busy."

I thank her and make good on my promise to call Fletch the moment I walk in the door. I fall on my sword and apologize to the best of my ninth-grade abilities (some of it may have been melodramatic with a trace of bullshit, yes, but it was no doubt heartfelt as we would marry some twenty years later).

She forgives me, and all is forgiven. Shane, come home!

And come home I do.

With the love of my life back in the black and my golf noodle in fine working order, one week after carving the 49, I knife a fine, windswept 39, curling in a tricky four-footer to break 40 for the first time ever. When my mom hears the news she immediately calls Freddie, and the next night he's on our doorstep, loaded down with "fresh-off-the-boat, flown-in-this-morning pompano." In his free hand are two cans of Borden's half and half whipping cream.

"You hungry? You love to fish so I know you love to eat 'em. This here's *Florida* pompano, man. Compliments of Chef Clark."

I later learn Chef Clark is Augusta National's head chef, and served many a meal to founder Clifford Roberts, including his all-time favorite, roast leg of lamb and slow-roasted oven potatoes. Before my mom can react, Freddie has taken over, standing over her stove with grease sizzling in the pan and his big hand dipping the fish in a mixture of half and half and salt and pepper. He sprinkles the pompano with flour and smiles.

And what a smile it is.

"It's a secret Augusta recipe, man. But it's so simple the members wouldn't believe me if I told 'em."

I believe him.

When the first piece of pompano hits the grease and starts crackling, Freddie turns to me with a wide grin and bright eyes. "Look at you, Mr. Golf Team. I want to hear *all* about it."

I fish the wadded scorecard out of my pocket and lay it on the counter.

"It's a long story," I say.

"I got plenty of time," says Freddie. "Plenty of time."

I had a week, I say to myself.

And what a week it was.

14

RETURNING THE FAVOR

I'm in the kitchen eating a Popsicle when the phone rings. Pop answers it, and I can tell from the tone of his voice it's a colleague, though the need is not serious nor life-threatening, as so many of Pop's calls are.

"Sounds great," says Pop into the receiver. "No, I wouldn't worry about buying him anything expensive. Not until you're sure he's serious about it. Does he play other sports? He does? That's good. The more well-rounded the better."

Pop stays silent for a minute. I have no idea who he's talking to or what they're talking about, but he's definitely got my attention.

"I wouldn't waste my money on that," says Pop. "Anything cut down will do just fine. If he gets serious about the game, then you can make the investment."

Serious about the game? Make the investment? It's a déjà vu, except the voice is Freddie's, not Pop's.

Those clubs are yours for as long as you need them, man. But when you're done with 'em, give 'em to someone who'll appreciate 'em just as much as you did.

I wave my hand to get Pop's attention. He shakes his head, as if to let me know he's still on the phone, to give him a minute to finish. I shake mine, too, then mouth the words "Walter Hagens."

Pop shrugs his shoulders. "Hold on a sec, Charles. Tripp thinks he's Marcel Marceau." He turns to face me. "What is it, Smoke? I'm on the phone."

"Sorry to interrupt, Pop. But the Walter Hagens are in the shed collecting dust. They'd be perfect for whoever you're talking about. He's a kid, right?"

A light goes on and my Dad smiles.

"Charles," he says. "What are you doing right now? Great. Can you come over in, say, thirty minutes? I think I've solved your problem. Bring little Charlie with you." Pop hangs up the phone and puts his hands on my shoulders.

"What a great idea, Tripper. Mighty generous, too." He tousles my hair. "C'mon. Let's go shine up those bats."

I hurry to the sink in the laundry room, get the hot and cold balanced just right, and lather up the scrub brush. Pop hands me the clubs one at a time, and I methodically dig the dirt out of the grooves. With the clubhead shining like a ray of hope, I bring my attention to the grip, scrubbing until it's tacky again, just like Freddie taught me. Pop dries off the last of the Hagens, slides the 9-iron into the bag as a car pulls up in our driveway.

We go outside, the bag slung over my shoulder.

After brief introductions, Pop turns to the kid and says, "What do you say? Show us what you got."

It's a good-natured question, but I can tell the kid is nervous. I'm nervous, too. I tee up a pinecone in the grass and hand him the 9-iron. Without saying a word, little Charlie draws back the Walter Hagen like he was born to do it, and I stare in disbelief as he drills the pinecone down our driveway with one of the prettiest swings I will ever see.

Autopilot takes over and I hand little Charlie—Charles Howell III, who will one day go on to play the PGA Tour and become one of its brightest stars—his very first set of golf clubs.

Freddie's voice is strong in my ear, and I tell little Charlie, "These are for you, man. For as long as you need them. But when you're done with 'em, give 'em to someone who'll love 'em just as much as you did."

Pop's hand is on my shoulder as we watch them drive away, and I can tell he's proud of me.

I'm kinda proud of me, too.

PART II

COMING OF AGE AT AUGUSTA NATIONAL

15

THE OFFERING

Freddie's in our driveway, kicked back in his old Buick. The driver's side door is open, his leg sticking out like a kickstand. Pop's on his way home from the hospital, and though I invited Freddie inside, he said he was fine waiting right here.

Now I know why.

"Hey man. You want a job?"

I'm fourteen, and I've never had a real job. But I avoid real jobs like the plague. My job, I convince myself (and somehow my parents), is to hone my craft, work on my game, practice, practice, and then practice some more, for surely a lucrative career awaits me on the PGA Tour.

Freddie snaps his fingers. "You in there, man? The job. You want it? And I ain't talking about making change for a pack of Nabs and a Goo Goo Cluster, or picking up trash in a plastic yellow suit. I'm talking about working on the golf course."

"What course?"

"Augusta National, man. What other course is there?"

I can't argue with that.

"Sure," I say, excited but with no idea what this job will be. "It sounds great. Would it be like an after-school thing?"

"Naw, man. I'm talking about Masters Week. Special situation. Created just for you."

"Sounds great," I say, waving as Pop pulls in the driveway in his white Volkswagen, a '64 Karmann Ghia with black leather seats and a faded paint job.

Pop points a finger at Freddie and smiles as he pulls into the garage.

Before Pop can get out of the car, Freddie turns to me and says, "Have your mama call me on Friday before she brings you out. I'll clear it with the gate."

"I'm on it," I say. "Thanks, Freddie."

I have no idea what I'm getting into and I don't care. It involves Freddie Bennett and the Masters, and that's all I need to know.

Friday rolls around and my mom makes arrangements. Freddie wants me there by four o'clock, so the moment I get home from school I grab a quick snack of peanut butter on a spoon and run out the door. A left here and a right there and soon we've turned down Magnolia Lane, one of the most hallowed drives in all of golf.

I've never been down this road except with Freddie, and it will be much later in life before I realize how privileged a ride it is.

The big guard waves and we wave back, not realizing he meant for us to stop, not tool on down like we own the joint. He steps out from his perch, and all I can see is the gun on his hip, big as a bazooka, chrome shining out of a black leather holster.

"Stop the car, Mama."

"What's wrong, shugah?" She turns to see what I see and slams on the brakes. "Oh, hello. I'm Marion Bowden, and this is my son, Tripp. We're here to see Freddie. He said he would call the gate and let y'all know."

"He did," says the burly guard, his hand closer than I'd like to what I know is a very loaded gun. "Just stop for me next time you come through these gates. *Please*, ma'am."

My mom promises the guard she will (I later learn his name is Magnum, and it's not because he drinks champagne) and steers her blue Cadillac de Ville down Magnolia Lane. We park where the members park—Freddie said it was okay—and walk to his office, an office that also doubles as the bag room. Mama walks in first and when Freddie sees her he stands up, rising from one of the biggest chairs I've ever seen.

"Hey, Mrs. Bowden."

"Hi, Freddie. How are you?"

"I'm good, I'm good." Freddie packs out a Marlboro Red but doesn't light it. He turns to me. "Hey, man, you ready to get signed up?"

"Sure," I say.

"You can wait right here, Mrs. Bowden. We won't be long. Take a load off." He points to his chair.

I follow Freddie out of his office and into an E-Z-GO, just like the one he took me fishing in. But this one doesn't have the governor removed, and it creeps in comparison.

We stop in front of a temporary trailer in the main parking lot. It's a Masters-only setup, and when the Monday after the tournament rolls around, it will be gone before lunchtime.

Freddie knocks and opens the door in one motion. "Anybody home?"

A short man with sea-blue eyes springs up with a quickness that surprises me.

"Hey, hey, Freddie," he says. "What brings you out here slumming?"

"I got you a forecaddy. For the job on two green. The one we talked about."

Pause. Crickets chirping.

"Last week," says Freddie.

"Oh, yeah. Yeah—I remember." Blue-eyes turns to me, hands on his hips. "How old are you, son?"

"Fourteen. Fifteen in November."

Wrong answer.

"Hmm. The cutoff is sixteen for working on the golf course. But I could get you in concession. They make pretty good money for just shuffling drinks and snacks."

"Me and my manners," says Freddie, half laughing. "Ed Johnson, Tripp Bowden. Ed, this here's my doctor's son."

I can see Ed's wheels are turning.

"This is Joe's kid?"

Freddie nods.

"Well, why didn't you say so? Come on over here Tripp, and let's get you signed up. Stand on that blue tape and let me snap a quick picture, get you that ID."

Freddie nudges me forward and two minutes later we're back in the cart. A picture ID that reads *Tripp Bowden, Forecaddy, Masters 1982* is in my hot little hand, the laminate glistening in the sun. Freddie's signature is in the corner. I rub it with my finger.

"You know the golden rule, don'tcha?"

I shake my head.

"Them that's got the gold makes the rules," says Freddie, a canary-eating grin on his face as we pull out of the parking lot.

I'm thinking Freddie's got more gold than Midas. He certainly has the touch.

16

BACKSTAGE PASS

It's the first full week in April, Masters Week, and I'm sitting on a bench in the caddy house, lacing up a pair of fresh out of the box green and white FootJoys. The shoes are custom-made for Augusta National, caddies in particular.

This is the first year someone who's not a caddy gets the privilege of slipping them on.

That someone is me. Me and two others, a veteran Augusta caddy named Tip Lite and another kid who is a couple years older than me. I figure he must have some pull, though I never get around to asking how much.

Outside I retrace the cart steps from my ride with Freddie, and twenty minutes later I'm slipping under the yellow ropes and taking my position behind the 2nd green. The one Freddie drove onto from the Bobby Jones sundial wearing bedroom slippers.

It's a different sort of job, this forecaddying. My assignment is to fix player's ball marks and sweep sand off the green with a fiberglass pole after they blast out of the bunker. Sounds dull as Parcheesi at first glance, but I feel like the guy who feeds the dolphins at Sea World. It's a menial job, but once you're on stage you get as many eyes on you as the Golden Bear himself.

There's no feeling quite like it, being not two feet from the likes of Nicklaus, Palmer, Player, and Watson, fixing their ball marks as they approach the green to raucous applause. Some players seem to appreciate us, some act as if we're not even there.

Palmer always says thank you.

Two years ago I had no idea who he was. Today I know him as the King. And the King just acknowledged one of his court jesters.

Good stuff, this. But as good as this is, it's not nearly as good as what awaits me after my job is done for the day.

Freddie's office.

Freddie's invited me to come by after I'm done, but only if I want to. My forecaddy ID gives me all-day and all-week access to Augusta National, the most revered golf course in the world. And to the Masters, the most elusive ticket in all of sports.

I understand if you want to take a rain check.

Rain check, my ass.

An invitation to Freddie's office blows everything else out of the water in ways you could never imagine. When the last group putts out I tell my fellow forecaddies I'll see 'em tomorrow. Walking towards the clubhouse, I repeat Freddie's words like a mantra.

Walk up to the pro shop like you belong. Push back your hat so the Pinkerton can see your eyes. Look dead into his and say, "I'm here to see Freddie." Don't miss a beat and don't slow down. Walk in like you own the place.

I do as I'm told, only to later realize all I ever need to do to access almost anything at Augusta is mention five simple words: *I'm here to see Freddie.*

After thanking the Pinkerton, I walk down the short path around the side of the pro shop, squeak open the door to Freddie's office. A tall, good-looking Spaniard is standing over Freddie's desk, talking in broken English. He would win the Masters that year, after a rain delay that pushed the tournament to Monday, beginning his final round 3, 3, 3.

Birdie, eagle, birdie.

Freddie sees me, nods, and flicks his wrist, the sign to come in. He gets up from his chair and gestures to it with an open hand and so I sit down. The Spaniard looks at me like I just walked on water. He turns to Freddie, asks about changing out his grips. Had Freddie ever done that before?

Freddie nods and says, "Yes, sir. All day long."

Under his breath I hear something else, but I can't quite make it out.

The Spaniard shakes Freddie's hand, thanks him, and leaves.

When the door bounces shut, Freddie opens his hand and a five-dollar bill falls onto the floor. He laughs.

"Ain't that something? That sonofabitch wants me to re-grip his clubs and he gives me five bucks—*five bucks* to make sure they're ready for tomorrow!" He's really laughing now. "But I'll do it. Ain't no doubt about that." Freddie reaches into the Spaniard's bag and pulls out his driver. "Hey, this feels pretty good. Got it balanced just right."

The fiver is still lying on the floor.

He hands me the driver. I stand up, grip it, and waggle. I'm in awe as much as I am dumbfounded, but Freddie's right. This club feels great.

"So, how'd it go, man? You make out all right?"

"It was awesome," I say, and then I tell him how Chi Chi Rodriguez poked me with his putter and asked if I was Frank Beard's son (I had no idea who Frank Beard was) and how Arnold Palmer thanked me for fixing his ball mark. Looked me right in the eye.

"You mean this guy?" asks Freddie, in a voice only I can hear.

In walks the King himself.

"Hey, Freddie," says Palmer as the two men shake hands. "Always good to see you."

"Always good to be seen," says Freddie, "especially at my age." Palmer laughs, and they talk about things that don't pertain to me, don't pertain to golf. I stand there in pure disbelief, not three feet from the man who, through television and his amazing charisma, changed the game of golf forever.

Just like with the Spaniard, I can feel Arnie's eyes on me, wondering who I must be, given access to this mother of all backstage passes.

"This here's my doctor's son," says Freddie, as if reading Arnie's mind.

The look on his face says he has a vague memory of me, but nothing clicks. He smiles a hello, turns to Freddie, back to me, then Freddie again. He says something about him and his 4-iron no longer being friends, then pulls the iron out of the bag and grips it.

What a grip! If God had hands they would be Arnie's. Wrapped around a golf club they look like something off a wall in the Sistine Chapel. No wonder they call him the King.

Arnie slips the 4-iron back in the bag, tells Freddie he'll see him tomorrow, and walks out, waving as he goes.

"Check this out," says Freddie as the door shuts. He hands me Arnie's 4-iron. The clubface has his name on it. "Grip it, see what you think."

Are you kidding me? Grip Arnold Palmer's 4-iron?

But grip it I do, and the leather grip feels sticky and smells like earth. Not dirt, but the big ball you're standing on.

"This is real golf here, man. How the game was meant to be played. Leather grips, iron shafts, and a ball that won't fly to hell and gone." Freddie looks at me, looks through me, comes back to himself, and reaches for the 4-iron. "Come over here," he says. "Got something I want you to see."

What could possibly top this?

17

LEARNING FROM A 1-IRON

It's surreal being in Freddie's office during the Masters, where it's often quiet as a cathedral, a sharp contrast to what lies outside the door. I look around the magic room. It's not lost on me that I am surrounded by the tools of the trade of the best golfers in the world, past and present.

There's Snead and Nelson, Palmer and Player, Ballesteros and Watson. And of course Jack Nicklaus, arguably the greatest golfer of all time, even with Tiger on the way. And then there's me, the opposite end of the spectrum. Yet here I am with my hand on the living legend's golf bag, a green and white MacGregor that looks heavy as a liquor barrel.

"Get your goddam hands off them clubs, boy! Don't nobody touch Jack's clubs but *me*!"

Nicklaus's caddy, an Augusta veteran named Willie Peterson with five Masters victories to his credit, storms over and almost knocks me down. Equally as quick, but with words and not actions, is Freddie.

"It's all right, William," says Freddie. "He's with me."

"With *you*?"

I can tell Willie is having trouble understanding what a skinny white boy like me is doing in Freddie's office with his hand resting on, of all things, Jack Nicklaus's golf bag.

"With you?" says Willie once again, this time more as a statement than a question.

Freddie nods, and that's all it takes to send Willie packing.

"All right, then." Willie turns and walks out the door, closing it gently with his fingers so it doesn't slam.

"Don't mind Willie," says Freddie. "He's a damn good caddy, just a little overprotective. All music but no dance." Freddie reaches into Jack's bag and pulls out the famous 1-iron. It's thin as a butter knife and looks more like something you'd carve a turkey with than a weapon capable of sending a golf ball 275 yards down a fairway.

"Put your mitts on this one and tell me what you think."

First Palmer and now Nicklaus. This is almost too much.

I gently place Jack's 1-iron in my hands, wrapping my fingers reverently around the grip.

"Well?"

"Wow!" I say. "It's so different than Palmer's."

"In what way?"

"It's thinner. Skinny. Almost feels smaller than a regular grip."

"Could be. Nicklaus has small hands. Lots of folks—I won't mention any names—thought he could never be any good, least not on a consistent basis, with hands that little."

"They were wrong about that."

"'Bout as wrong as you can get," says Freddie, smiling.

I grip the 1-iron again, in pure, still-a-kid disbelief that I am holding the best club in the bag of the greatest golfer in the world. Imagine strumming Hendrix's guitar or holding Babe Ruth's bat. Putting your hand in Willie Mays's glove or your head in Johnny Unitas's helmet.

I waggle once, twice, before handing the knife back to Freddie.

He shakes his head. "You do the honors, man. I bet you got some caddy in you."

I ease Jack's 1-iron back into his bag as gently as you would a newborn into his crib.

"Just goes to show you," says Freddie, wiping my fingerprints off the clubface, "that even the best golfer in the world isn't as perfect as he might appear." Freddie points his finger, as much at me as at the room. "You ain't gotta be perfect to succeed."

That's good news for me.

18

PERFECT PRACTICE

During my sophomore year of high school, my golf game stalls. I get no better, I get no worse. I'm breaking 80 more often than not, but throwing way too many 84s into the mix.

I don't know much about life on the PGA Tour, but I know it doesn't include many rounds in the 80s.

Freddie's voice is in my head: *Two things that don't last, man: dogs that chase cars and pros that putt for pars.*

But as he does for everything, Freddie has an answer for my golf game. His name is Mike Shannon, the former Augusta National assistant who gave me my first real golf lesson. A player in his own right, Shannon can also count as a claim to fame a certain college roommate who won the Masters on his first try—Frank Urban Zoeller. You know him as Fuzzy.

The summer of '81 finds me in the sleepy little town of Tupelo, Mississippi. Elvis was born here, and looking around I see little has changed since he first donned the blue suede shoes. I don't really want to go (who wants to go to Tupelo?), but Freddie insists.

"If you ever hope to realize your potential, Mike is the man. Can't nobody lay your cards on the table like him. Not big as a minute but can knock the ball into next week. Trained under a cat named Harvey Penick, who just so happened to teach the game to a couple young bucks named Ben and Tom. Last names Crenshaw and Kite. Mike knows his stuff. Listen to him, okay?"

Do I ever.

Mike Shannon is a big believer in practice, but not just any practice. Mike calls it perfect practice, the theory being that when you're faced with a similar situation on the golf course, you expect to be successful.

I like this theory. But not at first.

With the Mississippi sun beating down like a boxer, I spend my summer on a baked-out putting green, rolling three-footers until I can make fifty in a row. Miss one and start over, even if it's number forty-nine.

Grass dies under my feet until I get it right.

Three-footers are just the beginning. Make ten putts in a row from five feet. Two in a row from ten. Hole a twenty-footer before you can move on to the next level. Dig down into the bunker, the sun's reflection like a fun house mirror. No escaping until you've holed one out. Might be on the first swing, might not be until sunset.

Might not be at all.

Matters not. Only thing that does is getting back into that sweltering pit at 7:00 A.M. the next day, hitting bunker shot after bunker shot until one finally disappears.

It's a pain in the ass sometimes, but by week's end there is no denying perfect practice works perfectly. My putting and sand play are now the best parts of my game, the last to leave when the others fly south for the winter.

The night before my flight back to Augusta, I call Freddie with fingers so swollen I can hardly punch the numbers. The line rings twice, then a third time before Freddie answers. I'd rather tell him in person, but I know I won't be able to sleep if I don't tell him now.

"Hey, Freddie. It's Tripp."

"Hey, man. What's shakin'? You learning a lot, ain'tcha? Things about the game you never knew existed, I bet. Told you Mike knew his stuff."

"Mike's great," I say, and I go on to tell Freddie all about perfect practice, not knowing he's heard it all before.

Freddie lets me talk.

"You sitting down?" I ask.

"I am now."

"I shot seventy four today! Best round ever. I hit fourteen greens. Can you believe it?"

"That's great, man. How many birdies?"

"Four," I say. "Three on the back nine. One I made after my second shot bounced off a tree and onto the green. It almost rolled in for an eagle!" I'm so excited I can hardly breathe. "I mean, what are the odds of *that* happening?"

There's a short pause on the other end.

"Apparently, they're pretty good," says Freddie, laughing. "Come see me when you get home, all right, man?"

I tell him I will, of course I will. Then I do something I should've done long ago.

"Freddie?"

"Yeah, man?"

"Thanks."

"For what?"

"For everything."

"Don't thank me. Thank Mike. And fly safe, all right?"

I promise I will and we say our goodbyes. I hang up the phone and stare at fingers so swollen I can't close my hand. I have calluses on my calluses, the sun's fist print on my face. Every muscle in my body aches and I could sleep standing up if given half a chance.

Man, do I feel great.

19

EVEN PAR, 72

Time flies no matter what your age, but when you're a kid it straps itself to rocket ships.

My first Masters as a forecaddy ends far too soon, but spring fever and a bad case of acne are enough to get my mind on other matters, important or otherwise. I fall in love, lose my virginity, smoke my first cigarette, crack open my first beer. I also shoot par for the first time, using the same golf ball all the way around. A Kro-Flite, of all things, as I had run out of Titleists the day before and knew if I charged another sleeve of balls in the pro shop my mom would have my ass.

Freddie and Pop are sitting at the kitchen table when I come in, the sun long a memory in the fading summer sky. My pink shirt is stained with sweat and white patches of salt. I smell like I've been running track.

"Hey Tripper, what's shakin'?"

"Hey Pop. Hey Freddie."

Freddie swishes his glass and looks me over. "Man, that's a shit-eatin' grin if I ever saw one,"

I can't hold back another second.

"I shot par for the first time today," I say, grinning like a circus clown. "With this." I toss the Kro-Flite to Freddie. It disappears in his huge hand.

"Kro-Flite? Man—you don't see these around anymore. Where'd you get this thing?"

I shrug. "It just showed up in my bag."

"Shooting par with a Kro-Flite," says Pop. "No more Titleists for you." He looks at Freddie and laughs.

Freddie tosses back the Kro-Flite, reaches under his chair, and pulls out a dozen Titleist balatas. He hands me the box, black with raised gold letters. I don't need to open it to know the numbers are red, six through nine.

My favorite numbers.

"The game's all about distance and control, man. But if you ain't got control, all the distance in the world won't do you a damn bit of good."

"So *that's* what I've been doing wrong," says Pop.

"Congratulations," says Freddie, offering his hand. "I'm proud of you, man."

We shake.

"Thanks," I say, holding the box of Titleists like it's my first Christmas. I pull out a sleeve and rattle it. "Wait a minute. How'd you know? Nobody was out there but me. I played by myself."

"Man, I know *everything*," says Freddie, looking me in the eye as he sips his finger of scotch.

I'm beginning to believe him.

20

HUNDRED-DOLLAR HANDSHAKES

The Masters years fly by, each one faster than the last. I blink and I'm seventeen, with graduation staring me in the face. So much has changed since I first donned the forecaddy uniform, but one thing hasn't, and I pray it never does.

Freddie's office during Masters Week.

Inside the yellow ropes and behind Augusta National's very closed doors, I've had the catbird seat to a slew of daily appointments with the world's richest, most powerful men, and without a doubt the greatest players in the game. I'm luckier than most, having met players like Tom Watson (up close his arms really do look like Popeye's), Chi Chi Rodriguez, Seve Ballesteros, Ben Crenshaw, Nick Price (back when he was the number one player in the world—people forget that), Greg Norman—too many great players to list. And while they don't always offer a handshake, they always offer acknowledgment. Freddie introduces me as "his doctor's son," and they greet me with a look on their faces that says, "This kid must be somebody special, because Freddie doesn't let just anybody sit in his chair, much less some punk-ass kid."

With Freddie, it feels great to be a punk-ass kid. I want to stay this way forever, and at least for today I can. It's Masters Sunday, 1984, with the tournament winding down.

"Hope they got a coat small enough to fit him," says Freddie, pointing to the TV. "He's a little thing but man can he roll it. That cat's made more putts than Carter's got liver pills."

The Augusta member sitting on the edge of Freddie's desk shakes his head like a sprinkler. "Where do you come up with these things, Freddie?"

Freddie taps his head with a ballpoint pen. "Got a million of 'em," he says, smiling.

The member, a powerfully rich man, lays his eyes on me hard—not in a mean way, just intense, as if he's thinking. *Freddie's doctor's son, eh? Must be one hell of a doctor.*

I forgot to mention I'm sitting in Freddie's chair. I tried to get up, but he waved me off.

"Okay, Freddie," says the member. "It's almost time for the presentation, and I've got to coordinate an interview with the low amateur—but what are you gonna do, right?" He downs his vodka tonic, pulls out the lime, and chews. "But I think you're right, Freddie. Crenshaw's finally going to win a major. We got the best greens in the world—makes sense the best putter in the game would break through here. I've always liked Ben, truth be told. Hell, I'm a Texan too!"

Freddie nods in agreement before giving the member one more Augusta story, as only Freddie can tell them:

"It's the Masters in '53, the year Hogan won all the majors he played in. Just a few years after he almost got killed by that damn bus. He didn't play in the PGA, but not by choice. Back then they scheduled the British Open the same time as the PGA—the PGA wasn't considered as big a deal as it is now. It was still a major, but one you could take or leave. The change in attitude—you can thank Arnie for that." Freddie looks at me and grins. He knows what I'm thinking.

I've heard this story before.

"It's the second round, and Hogan booms a drive down the left side of 15 fairway, the green an easy reach in two. But Hogan lays up. There's a rookie in the group behind him, a Masters first-timer, green as a spring onion. He hits a pretty good drive himself, about twenty yards to the tee-box side of Hogan's. When he gets to his ball, he's surprised to see Hogan walking over the Sarazen Bridge with a wedge in his hand. Meaning, of course, Hogan had laid up in spite of the big drive.

"After Hogan's group finishes, the rookie rips a 4-wood onto the green, clearing the pond with ease. On in two, putting for three. A chance for eagle, right? But he's just shaking his head: Why in the world would Hogan lay up with the green in easy reach?"

The member leans in, hanging on Freddie's every word like a kid listening to ghost stories. All that's missing is a full moon and a hoot owl.

"After the round, with Hogan coming out of the scorers' tent after signing his scorecard for a sweet little sixty eight, the kid stops him—something you never, ever do to Hogan. But the kid does right and apologizes, calls him Mr. Hogan and not Ben, says may he please just ask him this one question. Hogan just stands there. Doesn't say yes, doesn't say no. The kid goes ahead and asks: 'Mr. Hogan, I couldn't help but notice, but over on fifteen. Your drive, sir. It was well past mine. Twenty yards or more. Mr. Hogan, the green was certainly within reach, yet you laid up. I hope I'm not out of line in saying this, but I must, as I'm trying to learn this game the only way I know how. Mr. Hogan, you're the best player on tour. Reaching that par 5 in two would have been a piece of cake for you.'

"Hogan says nothing, just stares the kid down, lights a cigarette, and takes a pull. With smoke curling from the corner of his mouth, Hogan looks the kid in the eye and says, 'I didn't *need* an eagle, young man. You, apparently, did. And for the record, I hate cake.'"

"*Daaaaaammmm,*" says the member, his mouth wide open. "What a story. That Hogan must have been something."

"Wouldn't piss on you if you were on fire," says Freddie.

The member stands up. I can see he's holding his right hand in an odd fashion, like he can't pull his fingers from his palm. He offers this suddenly crippled hand to Freddie, who shakes it like you might see a preacher shake hands with the deceased's family after a funeral.

He cups it.

When the member leaves, waving with his no-longer-crippled hand, Freddie opens his and a neatly folded bill falls onto his desk. It's folded so tight I can't tell the denomination.

"Open it," he says.

"Whoa," I say, staring at Ben Franklin. "That's a hundred-dollar bill!"

"A *cat eye*," says Freddie. "But he looks lonely. Better put him with his friends." Freddie reaches into his pocket and pulls out a wad of bills that could pass for one of those jelly rolls you see on a country road. He slides Ben Franklin into his rightful place and snaps the big rubber band.

"I got a tip for you, man."

"Sure," I say, my eyes big as the victory marble.

"A little tip goes a long way, but a big tip goes forever." Freddie smiles and slides the knot back into his pocket. "And forever is a mighty long time."

21

FIFTEEN WILL GET YOU TWENTY

Every golfer should see the Masters up close and personal at least once before they put on their last clean shirt (Freddie-speak for when someone dies). And if they're lucky enough to see it on Sunday, the Green Jacket presentation ceremony is not to be missed. The air is electric, the immortality of the green-jacketed champion undeniable. The made-for-TV presentation in the Jones Cabin is nice and all, but it doesn't come close to the real thing.

I'm watching the real thing right now, via a live, closed-circuit feed on the tiny TV sitting on Freddie's desk. It's just Freddie and me; most of the players' bags are gone—the ones that don't win something seldom stick around for the ceremony. Can't say I blame 'em.

"I gotta admit I wasn't sure the little fella was long enough to win here, but a ninety-year-old man could have broken eighty with all the putts Ben Crenshaw made," says Freddie. "He looked like Bobby Locke out there."

I've come to appreciate Freddie's obscure references in conversation. Not many people would know Bobby Locke if he rose from the dead and started signing autographs at Barnes & Noble. But I know exactly who Locke is—the best putter of his generation, just maybe the best putter the game has ever known.

I know because Freddie made sure of it.

If you just play the game and don't study the game, you'll never be a complete golfer. You ain't gonna change the future if you don't know about the past.

I stare at the TV as a handsome Spaniard slides the Green Jacket on 1984 Masters champion Ben Crenshaw.

"Another one for the books," says Freddie, reaching for the TV. For Freddie, when something is over, it's *over*.

Before he can switch off the tiny black and white, a slow-moving gent as old as the Olympics shuffles in with a blond on his arm. She's as smoking as a Boy Scout campfire, twenty if she's two, and sporting a pair of pink leather pumps with three-inch heels. There's not a bead of sweat on her, and though she's brown as a peanut, there's no doubt she hasn't stepped one foot on the golf course.

But what a foot it is.

"Quite a tournament, eh, Freddie?"

"Another great one for the books," says Freddie, repeating what he just told me. He starts to stand, but the old man waves him off.

"No need to stand for little Lisa here, Freddie. My daughter knows she's respected around here." The old man laughs, and Freddie blends in his corporate special.

"If that's his daughter, I'm the Kubla Khan," says Freddie in a voice meant only for me.

I swallow my laugh.

"Say, Freddie. I'm coming back down a week from Friday. Got some heavy hitters working on a merger for me, and they've done a damn fine job. I'll need some serious caddies—no bulls, okay?" He slides a fifty onto Freddie's desk, smiling and showing dentures as he pushes the bill under Freddie's hands, which just seconds earlier were folded.

"Yes, sir. Consider it done."

"Thank you, Freddie," says the old man, shuffling off with the aid of the long-legged blonde. "You always take good care of me."

He waves as they walk out the door.

"A McGarrett," says Freddie, lifting his hand off the fifty.

"*McGarrett*?"

"As in *Hawaii Five-O*. Tell me something, Tripp." Freddie points to the unlikely twosome as they disappear through the door. "Ever wonder why a dog chases a car when he knows he can't drive it?"

22

HOMECOMING

After graduation I turn the dial to college, the University of Georgia in particular. I've received no letters of intent from any school of interest, much less the powerhouse Bulldogs, but I'm hopeful that a good summer on the tournament circuit might sweeten the pot. Worst case scenario, I walk on. Happens all the time, right?

But that summer, like many of my summers, doesn't go exactly as planned, and I have little to show for my efforts except a victory in the West Lake Junior Club Championship (that and a dollar will buy you a Happy Meal) and a runner-up finish in the Frank Laporte Memorial. I guess I'm most proud of the Frank Laporte—a tougher field and for a good cause, keeping a kid's name alive after an untimely death in a car accident.

But the Laporte and the Junior Club Championship aren't on any school's radar, because they're local events, and as the summer winds down I find myself faced with a decision. Attend UGA and try to walk onto the team (not likely, truth be told) or hang up the competitive sticks and go dream about something else. I've played golf half my life, which you think would make me great and not just good, but somehow it hasn't worked out for me. It kind of snuck up, the finality of it all, and I can't help but wonder if I just spent the last eight years of my life wasting time. Sure, I can shoot a 72, but I can just as easily shoot an 80.

It's almost as if I'm afraid to succeed.

Georgia soon falls off my radar—too many people, too many parties, not enough self-discipline. Community dive Augusta College rears its ugly (or so I thought at the time) head, knocks on my door, and asks me to dance. She's the only game in town, so I'd be a fool to say no.

When Freddie hears I've bagged Georgia and opted for Augusta College, he tells me it's not a bad thing, not in the least. Nothing wrong with staying home a couple years until you figure out what you want to do. Trouble is, I thought I knew.

I thought I was meant to play golf.

A few phone calls later and I find myself on the 1st tee of Forest Hills Golf Club, nervous as a preacher with no sermon. The eyes of Augusta College's golf coach are on me, and I can tell he's wondering if I'm the savior of his golf team or just a waste of four hours.

A big, galloping hook into the trees has him thinking the latter, but when the ball cracks a big loblolly and lands back on the fairway, I breathe again and an unexpected wave of confidence washes over me. It's one of those times when you just know it's going to be a good day.

Turns out I was right.

I walk off the 18th green with a 75 in my pocket. Not Tour material, but not bad from the back sticks at sneaky-long Forest Hills, especially when you throw in the double bogey on 17. Coach turns to me before I can grab my bag and offers his hand.

"I really like your swing, and your attitude even more. Whoever taught you the game certainly knew what they were doing."

You like my swing?

"Keep up the good work, Tripp," he says, handing me the scorecard.

I take it like a consolation prize.

Coach snaps his fingers. "Oh, I almost forgot."

"Yes, sir?"

"Congratulations," he says, smiling. "You made the team."

23

MOST IMPROVED

A date with carpal tunnel syndrome my sophomore year turns four years of college into five, but I'll be damned if I'm going to complain. I'm all about postponing the inevitable, contrary to popular belief.

The inevitable. Sometimes in life we simply don't see it. Sometimes we see it but don't believe it. Other times it simply scares the crap out of us so we hide under the covers, hoping like hell it goes away.

All of the above applies to me.

Two sentences describe my college golf career, and it's as laughable as it is pathetic.

As a freshman, I was Player of the Year. (Good stuff, right?)

As a senior, I won Most Improved.

Not so good.

From Player of the Year to Most Improved. I'll let you chew on that for a bit. Use your imagination as to what happened during the years in between.

Four months after graduation, all I have to show for myself is a degree in English, a minor in psychology, what *should* be a major in philosophy because I took every course offered, and a refrigerator full of beer. But at least I have that, and I'm drinking one right now, so cold it hurts my teeth. There's also a cigarette dangling from my fingers. A Marlboro, with three drags left. I'm not a habitual smoker—two packs a month tops. If there's a monkey on my back, I hardly notice him.

My state of affairs and my direction in life are far more difficult to ignore.

Since graduation, my main source of income is renting out my bedroom for twenty bucks a day to a friend of a friend working at the local nuclear plant. Doesn't sound like much, but it adds up over time. How much do you need, really, when your get-up-and-go has got up and went? Long as I've got plenty of cold beer and the occasional Marlboro, I'm in pretty good shape.

Who am I trying to kid?

I close my eyes and make a laundry list, curious if there's anything worth cleaning.

Let's see: I dedicated my life to playing a game I was good at but not great at. Nothing wrong with that, but I did a pretty piss-poor job of leaving myself anything to fall back on. With a degree in English and minors in psychology and philosophy, I can either teach or stare out windows.

I'm way too big of a bullshitter to ever teach.

Life as a professional golfer? Though I lettered four years on a Division I golf team, I have as much business making a living swinging the sticks as I do running a marathon barefoot.

What else?

I've got a good girlfriend, sweet and pretty and I know she loves me. She's off at school—an all-girls college up North—so we don't see each other as often as we'd like. In spite of the absence, I wouldn't trade it for the world. There is a lot to be said for rediscovering one another.

Definitely worth cleaning, that one.

I'll never know why I didn't look into the business side of golf—working in a pro shop, teaching, selling sticks as a rep for Titleist or TaylorMade. I just didn't. Simple as that.

I live in a pretty shitty apartment. Brookside West, but we call it Brookside Hell. A family of fifteen lives next door to us, ranging from a toddler barely walking to a daddy who is always stumbling.

Not that I can cast a stone without casting one at myself.

I open my eyes and throw as hard as I can.

24

A GAME OF CATCH

Six beers and three false starts later, I pick up the portable and punch in the number for the Black Bat. Freddie answers on the first ring.

"This is Freddie."

"Hey, Freddie, it's Tripp."

"Hey, man. What's going on?"

I tell him what I just told you, that I feel like a failure because I've done nothing with my so-called college degree, that I wasted all my parents' money playing golf, knowing damn good and well I was never going to be good enough at it to even sniff the pro ranks. (This is actually not true—I always thought I had a chance, that one day things would click, and everything would just magically fall into place.)

Black magic is more like it. And me the voodoo doll.

There's silence on the other end, and I can hear Freddie's breathing.

"I got an idea, but I ain't so sure you're gonna like it. You're gonna *love* it! Hell, one of these days you're gonna thank me."

Since my prospects are zero, I tell Freddie I am open for anything.

"How 'bout a job caddying? Out here. Ain't like you've never done it before, but this time it'll be different. This time it'll be for real. No Sunday afternoon smashing grass for a bunch of locals. I'm talking sunrise to sunset, seven days a week, from the third week in October to the third week in May. I'm talking *for real*."

"I never thought about being a caddy. I'm not saying I'm above it or anything. Not in the least. It's just that I'm still trying to figure out what I want to be when I grow up." I wait for a laugh that never comes.

"Who knows? Caddying might help you do just that. For most of these guys out here it just gets them off the street, but it might get *you* on the biggest street of all."

It doesn't take me long to realize he's talking about Wall Street.

"You never know who you might meet out here, man. Some of the richest, most powerful men in the world play golf out here. And those are just the guests!"

If I wasn't buzzed, I might have told Freddie no. Caddying, at least *serious* caddying, sounded like a lot of work. Sounded like the potential to make a lot of money, too.

Who am I kidding? I could never tell Freddie no.

"What you waiting for, man? An engraved invitation?"

"I'll do it," I say. "Tell me the next step and I'll take it."

"Well, since I do all the hiring and firing, there won't be any need for an interview. I asked if you wanted to be a caddy, and you said yes. Sounds like a done deal to me. Why don't you come on out for picture day the first week in October. We do it Monday through Friday so we don't miss any stragglers. We'll take your picture, issue shoes, cap, and uniform, assign you a locker. And that'll just about do it. Can't promise a bag the very first day, but if you stick with me, I'll more than make sure you get your share of good bags."

"Good bags?"

"Good bags don't mean good players, man. A good bag is one that drops it like it's hot."

Tips. Now *that* I understand.

"No doubt I could use the money," I say, popping another beer. "All right, then. Guess I'll see you in October."

"I'm counting on it," says Freddie. "Oh, one more thing. Stop feeling so damn sorry for yourself. And stop saying you dropped the ball."

"But I did."

"Man, ain't nothing wrong with dropping the ball as long as you catch it before it hits the ground. See you next month, all right?"

"All right," I say, and I mean it. A smile makes its way across my face as I hang up the phone. I guess sometimes you don't realize how close you are to the edge until someone pushes you over.

Never thought I'd say this, but that's not always a bad thing.

25

HOW TO PAY THE FIDDLER

I pull away from my thoughts and I'm back at Freddie's gravesite, a dirt clod in my hand. I don't remember kneeling, and when I stand my knees creak, telling me I've been down here for quite a while. I'm not as young as I used to be (who is?), with forty staring me down like a martian from that Bugs Bunny cartoon.

Some leaves have fallen on Freddie's grave, and I swish them away before walking over to the impressive display of wreaths and ribbons. I recognize most of the names, one in particular which further accentuates the fact that Freddie Bennett could get next to and stay next to the most unlikely of people.

The display is almost twice my size, and I am not surprised to see it is from the chairman of Augusta National. This one has been personally sent. No "on behalf of" here.

I pull out a yellow chrysanthemum and start plucking the petals. She loves me, she loves me not. I had no way of knowing, lo those thirteen years ago when Freddie gave me my break into the caddy world, that he had set in motion a most unlikely course of life-changing events. Moving to New York City to pursue copywriting dreams (a chance to finally make something of my English degree), moving back to Atlanta where I start my own advertising agency, rediscovering and marrying my high school sweetheart, buying a home, putting down roots, welcoming new life into the world, raising a family, and, finally, this: remembering an old friend.

I realize for the first time I owe Freddie Bennett my life. I don't know where I would have ended up without him, but one thing's for sure: I wouldn't be here, and I wouldn't be me.

I close my eyes, failing miserably as I try not to cry.

PART III
HIGHER EDUCATION

26

OPEN FOR BUSINESS

The alarm goes off. I don't.

My roommate, who also has to be up at the crack of dawn, bangs on my door as if the apartment is on fire. I don't do so much as grunt acknowledgment.

"Get your ass *uuuuuuup*," she yells, banging again like a drunk on the door of a closed pub. But she's a morning person and there is sweet laughter in her voice.

Me? I am Midnight at the Oasis.

I roll over like an out-of-practice possum and slap the cheap Panasonic with a flailing hand, wishing it was a Bose. The time is 6:22; the sun is still at the tiki bar having a beer, and I'm wondering why the hell I set my clock for this ungodly hour.

And then I remember. Funny how you remember.

I never had a real job in my life, so I guess it was easy to forget this one.

As I sit up on my arms, I remember: I'm going to be a caddy, and today is my first day. At Augusta National, of all places. Me— the recent college grad with a degree in English and minors in philosophy and psychology—is gonna be a caddy. A rookie caddy; a.k.a. bag toter, grass smasher, bull.

I roll over again. But only to push my body into position to get out of the water bed, a Christmas present I begged and pleaded for only to find that I needed to put a tablet under my tongue in order to sleep through the night on it. Don't even think about having sex on the damn thing unless you're on leave from the Cirque du Soleil.

Okay, I'm up. The sun isn't, but I am.

I shower quickly, blow-dry the hair, slap on some gel to style the straight locks, and I'm off. Breakfast is an afterthought—seems way too early to ingest anything. The Trans Am fires up like a champ, and I pull her out of the confines of Brookside Hell and onto Berckmans Road for my two-minute drive.

Yes, I am that close. My apartment, hellhole that it is, backs up to Augusta National, and I think to myself that's pretty cool, even at 6:30 in the morning.

I turn onto Washington Road. Before I can accelerate beyond thirty, I hit my blinker and take a slow right turn.

Augusta National Golf Club.

Just like that I am inside the hallowed gates. I wave at Magnum, the old guard I've known since I was a thirteen-year-old punk kid. Magnum doesn't wave back but responds with a pounding fist on the trunk as I go straight down Magnolia Lane and not down Caddy Lane, the gravel road that runs behind the practice tee. I slam on the brakes. Had I hit one of the magnolias?

I won't repeat Magnum's words, which made me quickly realize I had *not* clipped a magnolia.

I back up with the tailpipe between my legs and turn hard right. A hundred yards later I'm in the caddy parking lot, although it's not really a lot—just a portion of Gate 10 the caddies use during the season to park their cars. There are no white lines, no arrows pointing which way to go. Just park behind the guy in front of you.

My black Trans Am sticks out like a prom dress at a hoedown.

Not many caddies have wheels, yet there must be twenty cars parked in the caddy lot, with every car toting two caddies or more. I make my way to the caddy shack, wondering if this was such a good idea after all.

I walk through the open green door, feeling like the kid in *Weird Science* when he walks into the Candy Bar and everything stops. I half wave, half smile, look desperately for a place to hide.

There isn't one.

Not that I'm Joe Popular, but it's rare for me to walk into a room and not know a soul. Truth be told, and I hope this comes out right, but it's rare for me to walk into a room and not own it. Not because I'm Greg Gregarious, but because I usually know enough people to get the energy going, the jokes going, the mood changing.

Here, the only mood changing is mine.

After the initial freeze frame, most of the caddies go about their business, except for one who looks awfully familiar, but for the life of me I cannot remember his name. He caddied for me once during Closing Week, and he sure remembers mine.

"Little Doc," he yells out. "Ol' Little Doc. What are you doing here?"

Damn good question.

Trying my best to feel out of place, I want to say. But instead I tell him the truth.

"I'm here to caddy."

"Say what?"

"Yeah, I know. Crazy." I shrug my shoulders. "I needed a job and Freddie gave me one, so here I am. Ready to walk those fairways, hike those hills." I look away, realizing how stupid that sounds.

"But you a college man. On the golf team. Damn good golf team. Ain't you going pro?"

"No," I say. "Not good enough."

"Little Doc, you can golf your ball."

"Don't want to waste Big Doc's money," I say. "May need to tap him later." I fake a smile.

The caddy laughs. I wish to hell I could remember his name. It's on the tip of my tongue but at the bottom of my brain.

"Well, I heard that! Your Doc's a good man. Damn good man. You got a good Daddy, Lil' Doc."

He's right. Pop is a good man.

"Well, lemme know if I can do anything for you. Hey, I gotta go. Gatorade Man got a group of twelve and we about to make us some money. Real money. Gonna walk our asses off to get it, though."

And just like that he was gone. And just like that I was alone again.

And just like that I smell butter beans. It smells like a family reunion.

"Hey man—you hungry?" A familiar voice calls out from behind a half-open window of the caddy-house kitchen. The window is made of steel bars and has been stuck for years. If you want to serve something to someone, you have to bend down to do it.

"Hey Freddie," I say, and then, thinking about his question I say, "Sure, I'm always hungry."

"How 'bout some butter beans and chicken?"

An odd choice for seven in the morning, but now that I'm awake I'm no doubt hungry. I reckon it's not much different than eating leftover pizza.

"Sure," I say, and three dollars and fifty cents later I'm sitting down on a long wooden bench—the kind you see outside a country church, trying not to spill a bowl of butter beans big enough to feed the five thousand.

I forgot to get something to drink, so I go back to the counter and order a Coke.

"Grape soda?" asks Horace, who I remember from my Closing Week days and Pop bringing me into the caddy house during the Masters. It comes out like one word.

"No," I say. "Coke. Please."

Horace scoops ice into a green Masters cup, pours in the liquid.

"Fifty cent."

I slide him the money, looking deep into my grape soda.

Back on the bench I pull wax paper off my chicken sandwich and open it up. A leg and a thigh. No wing. It's my lucky day.

I ate many of these as a kid, the good ol' bone sandwich, thanks to Pop's connections and my friendship with Freddie. Augusta National was a different world back then. Once you got the hall pass, you always had the hall pass.

I take a bite of butter beans, not at all surprised how good they are. Freddie has cooked them long and slow, with just the right amount of salt, pepper, and fatback. Freddie can flat-out cook. But unlike most Southern cooks, he knows grease doesn't have to mean greasy. Still, I can't believe I'm eating butter beans at seven in the morning. Better yet, I can't believe I'm *up* at seven in the morning. And maybe I'm not, since I feel groggier than a reentry astronaut.

Oddly enough my colon is wide-awake. Blame it on my gastrointestinal surgeon father who once told me one of the worst cancers you can get is colon cancer, and one of the leading causes is not taking enough shits. So me, I take more shits than a soldier takes leave.

Man, I gotta go. Gotta go *now*.

I stand up and look around, trying not to seem lost or confused. No bathroom in sight. I walk from the bench to the middle of the room, where I see what surely must be a bathroom, though there are no signs saying as much. I don't care. I have to go so bad it doesn't matter if it's a closet full of brooms.

I push open the door. Jackpot!

Or just pot. As in pots, crappers with no doors around them, newspapers scattered on the floor, urinals off to the left, a shower to the right. Not a door in sight. But I am about to ruin my day for good if I don't sit down, so I do just that. In front of God and everybody I do my due diligence, and as I'm kicking it into third gear I hear my name called, like in a bad third-grade dream when the teacher calls your name at roll call in the middle of the summer and you with a big fish on the line.

"Yo—you Tripp, ain'tcha?"

I recognize the face but the name escapes me.

"Yeah. I'm Tripp."

He takes off his hat like we're in a fancy restaurant. "It's me—Tip Lite. Remember? We worked together. On number two. Loooong time ago—back when Ballesteros could still find a fairway."

I put down the newspaper. "I remember you. Of course." And of course I did, but I was still half naked and trying to take a shit.

"What you doing here? It ain't Closing Week. You trying to caddy or something?"

What else can I say but the truth?

"I was looking for a job out of college and I talked to Doc and he said call Freddie, and you know Freddie so here I am."

"Well, all right," says Tip Lite. "Now ain't this something. Little Doc, caddying at Augusta National."

"Yeah, it's something all right," I say, looking around for toilet paper.

27

ENCYCLOPEDIA BENNETT

"Hey man, you got a minute?"

"Sure," I say, lifting my head off my chin. I've been staring at my shoes so long I've lost track of time.

"Come on," says Freddie. "Got something I want to show you."

I follow Freddie out of the caddy house. I can feel the eyes of many caddies on me as we hop in Freddie's golf cart and drive off.

"Got time for a crash course on Augusta National?" Freddie's big hands are on the wheel, and not for the first time do I notice how in control they are.

"Yeah," I say, not exactly sure what he means, but not particularly caring, either. I'm riding along the grounds of the most famous golf course in the world with the club's ambassador. Doesn't get much better than this, whether you love the game or not. Sure beats the hell out of sitting in the caddy house, waiting for a bag that may never come.

Freddie punches the gas, and we fly down one hill and up another. We crest the hill and stop, but Freddie doesn't get out so neither do I. He bows his head, but just for a brief slice of time's pie, like when you want a moment to yourself to remember an old friend or forget a bad memory.

"That's Mr. Roberts," says Freddie, pointing to a grove of what look to me like squatty dogwoods.

"They named a tree after Clifford Roberts?"

I can see Freddie hold back a smile. He shakes his head.

"That's where he's *buried*. Cremated. Just like he wanted. Buried on the place he built, also like he wanted. He told me that. Not long before he died."

"I heard Mr. Roberts killed himself. Is that true?"

Freddie ticks his tongue. "Depends on how you look at it. Mr. Roberts was eat up with the cancer. Just a matter of time, and he knew it, so he went out on his own terms. He was something else, Mr. Roberts. A damn good man. You always knew where you stood with him." Freddie points a thick finger into the cloak of dogwoods. "He's under that one. But don't tell just anybody, if you get me."

I get him.

"We got a bunch of members out here, man. Some say two-fifty, some say three. Only the chairman knows for sure, and he ain't telling. I got a pretty good idea, but I ain't telling either, unless you really want to know."

I shake my head. I'll save my chips for bigger secrets than how many members there are at Augusta.

Freddie rattles off names and occupations of various members at a rapid clip, so fast it takes me all the way to the letter M to realize he's listing them alphabetically!

The CEOs of Chevron, General Electric, Gannett Industries, Bechtel, Amoco—it's Fortune-500 company this and Fortunate-500 company that.

It is one hell of an impressive list.

As Freddie ticks off the names, he adds a quick blurb about each one, their likes and dislikes, the likelihood of getting a tip, getting paid well out the shop. This one only likes to play eighteen holes and the Par 3 course. This guy always plays forty five a day. This cat's a good one to get 'cause he'll just play nine but his guests will play all day, and he'll pay you what he pays the other caddies.

Freddie never once says a bad word about anybody.

I only wish I had a notebook. I'm deep in thought, trying to repeat the names and the idiosyncrasies that match each one, failing miserably. As if sensing my frustration, Freddie looks me in the eye and smiles.

"Don't sweat it, man. That's why it's called a crash course. You're gonna wreck every now and then."

I laugh, and as we drive by a grouping of buildings, Freddie names them one by one. "Ike's Cabin, Butler Cabin, Roberts Cabin, Stephens Cabin."

Freddie aims the cart down the 10th fairway, a huge drop of sixty-plus feet. By the time we reach bottom we're really flying. We stop when we reach the green, and Freddie locks the brake. He pulls a golf ball from his pocket, the hole cut dead center.

"If you forget everything I tell you today, that's okay. I can tell it to you again. But this won't be repeated." Freddie rolls the Titleist in his fingers, then in front of his face, as if it were a dart about to be thrown.

"The key to reading these greens is simple, just like most things in life are simple. It's all the over-education that makes things more complicated than they really are. Now, the key to reading Augusta's greens..." He leaves me hanging as he flicks the Titleist onto the slick surface. I watch in amazement as the ball rolls to the hole, bending right and damn near into the cup.

From forty feet away. Sitting in a golf cart.

"It's the grain man, not me. Grain'll put that ball on a leash and walk it like a dog!"

"That broke uphill!" I say, shaking my head. "A lot."

"You don't read Augusta's greens, man. You *remember* them."

You're right about that, I think to myself, knowing I'll never forget what I just saw.

I'm still weighing the improbable putting lesson when Freddie turns to me and says, "If you ever hear anybody call him 'Bobby' and they say they knew him, know this: They didn't know him very well."

"What's that?"

"Bob Jones, man. Cofounder of Augusta National. Ring a bell? His friends called him Bob, not Bobby. I laugh when I hear all the so-called big daddy journalists call him the great Bobby Jones. He was great, all right, but he wasn't no Bobby." Freddie rubs his hands on the steering wheel. "Gotta do your homework, man. Always, or you'll end up looking like a fool."

I promise Freddie I will.

We're on the 8th hole now, a reachable par 5 if you can crank it. We're parked around the back of the tee box and all I can see is a long slope of green.

"I got a thought," says Freddie, "and if I don't get it out I'll lose it. It's hell getting old, man. But it sure beats the alternative."

I've known Freddie long enough to know he forgets nothing. Name, rank, and serial number, and who you caddied for last Tuesday a year ago. I wouldn't say Freddie has a memory like an elephant. More like a computer.

"Close your eyes," he says. "I want you to use your imagination."

I close 'em.

"All right," says Freddie. "Imagine this good-looking green tee box is nothing but a slab of red Georgia clay, muddy as a pig pen from all the rain. Now imagine ol' Jones, call him Bobby or Bob—I don't care. That's between him and you if you consider yourselves friends. Now, imagine him on this tee, dressed as he always dressed, coat and tie, the plus fours. He's got the driver in his hands, and he's ripping tee shots into an even-muddier fairway covered in plowed-up tree stumps and wisteria vines. The whole place smells like fox fire and lavender."

"Fox fire?"

"Fancy word for tree root. Usually a pine, but not always. Cut it open before the sun goes down and it'll glow like a lightning bug and smell like Christmas."

My eyes are closed but my imagination is wide open. I can see and smell everything Freddie is saying.

"Any idea why Jones was knocking balls off a muddy tee box?"

I shake my head.

"To know where to put that."

I open my eyes, follow Freddie's pointing finger to a huge bunker guarding the right side of the fairway. Somehow I had missed it. Too busy looking at everything else, I suppose.

"Didn't need anything for the left side," says Freddie. "Those trees are thicker than the head of an ignorant man." He pops me on the knee. "That's something, ain't it?" he says, his eyes on the bunker, sand white as a Gulf Coast beach. "Wooden shafted driver, ol' piece of nothing ball that flew like a butterfly in a hurricane, and yet Bob Jones is ripping tee shots as far as most of the pros hit 'em now with all that newfangled equipment. Just goes to show you—it ain't so much the bat as it is the batter."

Freddie nods his head, as if convincing himself of something bigger than what he just told me.

"All right, man, we better hurry. Miles to go before we sleep."

Freddie clicks off the brake and punches the gas, steers the green E-Z-GO to the back nine. Our next stop is Amen Corner.

"I ain't gonna insult you by telling you what *this* is." He looks at me and I mouth the words *Amen Corner.* "But do you know how it got that name and who gave it to her?"

"No clue," I say.

"Cat named Herbert Warren Wind. Now there's a name for you. He was a journalist—wrote a pretty mean word now and again. No Shakespeare, but who is? He said these three holes—eleven, twelve, and thirteen—looked like hands praying. So he called her the Amen Corner."

"I like it," I say.

"Yeah, but I'm not so sure that's accurate. There's another one that says Wind saw the place like a piece of Heaven on earth, and just looking at it makes you want to shout from the Amen Corner."

I have no idea what that means.

"The Amen Corner. Like in the old black churches, where all the women and half the men shout 'Amen! Amen Brother!' as loud and as often as they can."

"Gotcha," I say.

"It's also a jazz tune—*Shoutin' from that Amen Corner!* Man to man, I don't really know which stories are true and which ones ain't. Herbert's long been dead, so it ain't like we can ask him. But it doesn't matter which story you believe, just so long as you've got one to tell. The more Augusta stories you got, the better chance at a tip. I wouldn't waste that one on a member, though." Freddie points to three towering loblollies left of the Hogan Bridge. "But this one, this one I'd tell all day long."

I slide to the edge of my seat.

28

DEM BONES

"You're joking," I say. "An Indian burial ground? At Augusta National?"

"Yes sir. Cherokee, so I'm told. Dug 'em up and moved 'em out like they were never even there. Bones, jewelry, coffins. All gone."

"Wow."

"Not all history is in books, you know."

Freddie rubs his knee. "I'm pulling your chain about the coffins, man. Cherokee didn't believe much in the box. Didn't want to trap the spirit, I reckon." Freddie slides a box of Marlboros from his pocket, lights one from a matchbook as green as the fairways, the Augusta National logo embossed in gold.

"You see those pines?" He points to the small grouping of loblollies left of the Hogan Bridge. "That's where you look for wind direction on twelve. Number eleven, too. Don't waste your time tossing grass in the air or looking at those trees behind the green. They won't tell you anymore about which way the wind is blowing than a bowl of ice cream."

"Got it," I say, again wishing for pen and paper.

Freddie points to 12 green. "See that creek? That's Rae's Creek. I used to swim in there when I was a kid—about the same age as you the first time I took you fishing."

There's a distant look in his eyes. It's hard for me to imagine Freddie as a kid.

"All right, man. Let's roll."

As we're riding down the 13th fairway Freddie tells me that this hole, considered by golf course architects and players alike to be the most natural golf hole in the world, was one of Jones's favorites. The winding creek was always there, and not a pocketful of dirt was moved to create the sloping terrain and hanging lies. A little hard to believe, but I don't care. I just love hearing Freddie talk.

We turn up 14, and Freddie points to where the tee shot should land, and what pins to never go for, even if I'm caddying for Jack Nicklaus.

"That pine," he says, pointing to the tree left of the green, "is a hell of a lot bigger than it looks. It'll catch your ball quicker than you can say 'double bogey.'"

I tell Freddie I can say it pretty fast, and we're both laughing as he pulls the E-Z-GO behind the tee box at 15.

"Lots of caddies tell their players to aim over there, but damned if I know why." Freddie points to the huge mounds guarding the right side of the fairway. "Guess they think it's a good place to bail out, but ninety-nine of a hundred balls that go over there stay right where they land. You ain't seen a hanging lie till you've been up there, man. Hanging like fat over a belt buckle."

I laugh, remembering my days as a punk kid, playing Augusta during Closing Week. I sent many a ball onto those hills, but not because I was aiming there.

Freddie drives the cart around the tee, not stopping until we crest the hill. It's a sharp drop-off to the green, eighty feet if it's an inch.

"Most important thing to remember on this hole is when and where to go for it. In two, in three, in I don't care how many. You got a guy up here with a 3-wood in his mind then put it in his hand. Most folks playing Augusta know they won't be coming back. They know it's the chance of a lifetime so don't ever tell 'em no, even if you're sure they couldn't get there with a bazooka."

Freddie looks me in the eye. I've never seen him so serious.

"Don't ever tell anybody to lay up on the chance of a lifetime."

29

FOUNTAIN OF KNOWLEDGE

"Okay," says Freddie. "Here's your deal maker, and I don't mean that fool out in the caddy yard. If this one doesn't get you a tip, that tip wasn't meant to be got."

We're parked behind the 4th green, my brain still crashing from the wave of information. Forty years of Freddie's knowledge of Augusta National crammed into one afternoon.

"The bamboo," says Freddie, pointing once again to the grove of skinny green trees that line most of the right fairway. "What's the rule?"

"Never go in there," I say. "No matter what."

"Say it one more time."

"Never go in there. No matter what."

"Good. Don't *ever* forget that one. There're snakes in there big as your leg, and they don't get to eat that often. I don't care if the club chairman knocks one in there, tell him to reload. If he has a problem with it, tell him to come see me."

I nod but I guess it's not convincing enough.

"I'm serious, man. Don't go in there unless you're following Jesus Christ."

"I won't," I say, and this time I'm serious, too, even with a smile on my face.

"We're on the same page," he says, hopping out of the cart. "Come check this out." Freddie motions to a water fountain directly behind the 5th tee. It's made of brass and looks old as Methuselah.

"You thirsty?"

I'm not, but I lean in for a drink anyway. I turn the handle but the water just dribbles out. The only way to get any would be to stick my mouth on the faucet. No way am I doing that. Not at Augusta National. I pull back.

"What's wrong?" asks Freddie, knowing exactly what's wrong.

"It's broken."

"Mr. Bowden," says Freddie, "a good caddy knows the only breaks at Augusta are on the greens and in the fairways. You mind?"

I back away. Freddie slides up to the water fountain, reaches into his pocket, and pulls out a tee.

"Exhibit A," he says, before sliding the tee tip-first into the front hole of the faucet. It's a perfect fit.

"After you," he says, motioning for me to take a drink. He turns the handle. A high stream of water finds my lips.

I'm shaking my head. "You're something else, Freddie."

"You right about that," he says, removing the tee. But instead of putting it back in his pocket, he hands it to me.

"Our little secret," he says.

I never tell a soul.

30

EIGHTEEN LESSONS

We're hightailing it down the 5th fairway when Freddie pulls a scorecard from his pocket. He hands it over and I open it, curious of the score inside. Course record, maybe?

Freddie grabs the scorecard and flips it over. On the back of the card are the names of the holes of Augusta National Golf Club.

He begins a monologue for the ages.

"All right, man. Hole number one. Tea Olive. Avoid the right hand bunker like the plague. It's deeper than a drunk philosopher. Haven't seen a four made outta there since Reagan was a boy. It's a half club longer than it looks, so make sure you account for it. Tricky green, but they're all tricky. Just make sure you got this thought at the front of your brain. Like I said, you don't read these greens, you *remember* them. So pay close attention to everybody's putt, even if your man can't play dead. Pay just as close attention to the other three cats in your group. You might be thinking that every time you go out on the track you've got just one chance to learn. Naw, man. You got *four chances*. And did I tell you to stay away from the pin when it's cut left? Chances of getting her close from there are slim to none, and pitch shots from the valley are for dead men. Grain runs hard towards eight green, so it's a lot, and I mean *a lot* faster than it looks.

"Hole number two. Pink Dogwood. Your line off the tee is just left of those right-hand bunkers. That creek running down the left side? It's only good for one thing, and that's eating Titleists. You can make five from the right woods, but not the left. If your man wants to go for the green, let him. Nothing wrong with being in those greenside bunkers. Easier pitch than being right in front of 'em. Grain runs towards that group of pines behind seven green. That means there are a bunch of putts that will break uphill. Good hole to earn your keep on, especially with first-timers. They won't believe you when you tell them it's breaking right.

"Hole number three. Flowering Peach. No sense in taking driver here unless your man is weak as a Shirley Temple and couldn't reach those bunkers with a hurricane behind him. Another one that's half a club longer than she looks. Lot better long than short. Up and down from that front swale is rare as snow in April, pro or no. Grain runs towards sixteen green, but if the scoreboard was up, I'd say it runs right at it.

"Hole number four. Flowering Crab Apple. I'll say it twice—you don't want your man in that front bunker. He might never get out. Long ain't wrong here. Grain's running hard left, where they put the grandstands during the tournament. Lot of ghost breaks here. Fact, there may not be a straight putt on this green outside a one-footer.

"Hole number five. Magnolia. Makes sense to name it that seeing as your line off the tee are those three magnolias on the far side of the fairway. Those bunkers on the left? Don't even think about going over 'em. I don't care if your man is long as *Gone With the Wind*, it just ain't worth it. If you do fly 'em, maybe you got half a club less in your hand. But the risk ain't worth the reward. If a bunker could take life and be rattlesnake-mean, that bunker would be it. This green is a beast, let's just leave it at that. You'll need to learn this one firsthand, just make sure you account for that false front. Adds at least half a club, though I know it doesn't look it. For the average Joe, five here is a pretty good score.

"Hole number six. Juniper. Don't let the valley fool you. Play the yardage on the card, and when the pin is on that top-right shelf, let it alone. I've seen some of the best players in the world ruin many a round going for that pin. Play for the middle of the green, take your three and run to the next box.

"Hole number seven. Pampas. As in the grass that'll slice your ass to ribbons if you try to squat down in it. Crazy ol' Donahue found out the hard way. Couldn't hold it, so he ran into the pampas to take care of business but it took care of him first. Lucky his ass didn't bleed to death. And I mean literally. So if your man hits one in there, hand him another. Don't even discuss it. Tee shot here is key—no need to hit driver unless he hits it so straight you could hang your clothes on it. Grain runs hard at that pine on the back of the green. The one on the right. This green gets a little tricky late in the day. Doesn't break as much as you think it would.

"Hole number eight. Yellow Jasmine. Named after the yellow flowering vines you see growing on those loblollies down the left side of the fairway. There's something blooming out here year round, regardless of the season. Did I say that already? Now that fairway bunker, stay out of it if you can help it. But if you do find your man in the sandbox, hand him a 7-iron. He'll still be able to get home in three. If he's got game, hand him the 5-iron. But nothing more than that. As you can see, there are no bunkers guarding the green. Not many par 5's out there hard as this one with no green-side bunkers. The green is who wears the pants on this hole. Anything longer than twenty feet, don't try to make it. Think three-foot circle and hope for a two putt.

"Hole number nine. Carolina Cherry. Tee shot here is pretty straightforward, and the only flat spot on the fairway is Roberts' Ridge, unless your man can boom it to the bottom. If it looks a little out of place that's because it is. Mr. Roberts had it built because that's where his drives always ended up and he couldn't hit off a hanging lie. True story. Doesn't affect the character of the hole because no pro ever hits it there. Ain't but a couple hundred yards or so off the tee. Now this green is nobody's friend. If the pin is on the front, shoot for the middle 'cause if you come up short of the flag there's a good chance she's rolling back into the divot you just took. Not that you want to miss a green, but if you miss this one make sure you miss it long.

"Hole number ten. Camellia. Let me make it clear that those are bushes you want to admire from afar. You get up next to a camellia bush and you may as well hand your scorecard to the janitor. Okay,

I like the drive here just right of center. The hill is steep and the kicks are sharper over there so she'll run like a sewer rat if you land her with a draw. The bunker at the bottom of the hill is way out of reach, really just for looks nowadays. Years ago that bunker guarded the green, but not so much since they moved it back. Speaking of bunkers, if the pin is cut right, stay left; no getting up and down from right of the flag unless you hole a thirty-footer 'cause that's about as close as you're gonna get from over there. Like you saw earlier, grain runs hard down to eleven tee box, and down grain putts here are some kinda fast. No shame in a five on this hole, tell you the truth.

"Hole number eleven. White Dogwood. Good hole to earn your keep on. When your man putts out on ten, hand him the driver and send him downhill. You keep walking to the fairway. They won't be able to see you from down there, so if you want to give your man's drive a little boost you can do it here. But I wouldn't kick it more than twenty yards or so. Also, you ain't heard a word of this from me. Now this fairway is wide enough to land a jet so down the middle suits just fine. Stay out of the left woods unless you want another six on your card. Right woods you have a chance. Left you have a chance, too—it's called *no*. Hogan used to say if you ever saw him on eleven green in two that means he pulled it. That just might be a true story. The pond on the left ain't big as a minute, but it's got more golf balls sitting on the bottom than Evel Knievel's got pain pills. Grain runs at the pump house. Not too many ghost breaks here.

"Hole number twelve. Golden Bell. One of my favorite holes. Remember what I said about the trees left of the Hogan Bridge. Look there for your wind direction and nowhere else. And if you see a caddy throwing grass in the air, slap it out of his hand. Club selection ain't as mysterious here as folks make it out to be. Pin in the middle and the yardage you see is the yardage you get. Pin on the right, add a club, not that I would want you going for that pin anyway. Pin on the left, drop back a club. Simple as that. Nothing wrong with being in the front bunker, but the back ones are a couple of junkyard dogs. Twelve is the flattest green on the course. Lots of straight putts on this one, so keep your memory book handy. It'll look like it just *has* to do something, but damned if it don't break so much as a nose hair.

"Hole number thirteen. Azalea. Just like on number ten, these are also bushes you want no part of. The creek running down the left side of the fairway is shallow as a prom queen, but you don't want any part of that either. Houdini couldn't make five from down there. The line off the tee is those cypress trees on your right. Fairway slopes left so it'll kick 'em back down to the middle. You can make five from the right woods, not the left. And if there's a flat lie on this fairway, I haven't seen it. If you got a guy who can really boom it let him go for it in two if the itch is strong, but it's a lot further than it looks, especially with the pin cut right. Trying to land a 3-wood on this green is like asking a Playboy Bunny out on a date. It might happen, but not very often. Grain here is running back to the tee box, maybe a little left of it, so there are some putts here that can break uphill. The pros don't mind hitting over this green, but I do. It ain't no picnic back there, man. I don't care what you got in your basket.

"Hole number fourteen. Chinese Fir. Might just be the toughest green on the golf course. Stay away from anything left. Right of center is your line off the tee, and the right woods aren't the end of the world. Like I said earlier, if the pin is left, leave it alone like it's got electricity running through it. Those pines guarding the left side of the green are nobody's friend, I promise you that. No matter what the yardage says here, tell your man to think half a club further, maybe more depending on his skill level. It's a rare up-and-down from in front of this green. From the back at least you have a chance. Grain runs hard toward eleven fairway, and man is she fast. Good hole to show 'em what you got. You might not believe it, but you'll see more forty-footers drop here than just about anywhere else on the course.

"Hole number fifteen. Firethorn. And yes, those mothers will stick your ass like a briar patch so stay away from the left side of the fairway. You don't want anything to do with those chocolate drops on the right, either. Plenty of room to roam on this one. No need to strain on the tee box. From the members' tees this one is reachable for a lot of players, especially when they get to their ball and see it's all downhill from there. Nothing wrong with being in the bunker right of the green, nothing wrong with being long either. I won't insult you by saying you don't want to be short. Take the yardage as it comes. Even though your approach is straight downhill, it pretty much plays what it plays. If you do tell your man to lay up here, try to keep him a hundred yards out, or whatever distance he hits full. It's soft as a jelly doughnut down at the bottom of that hill. Closer ain't better, if you get me. Grain runs hard towards the corner of the Sarazen Bridge. Putts tracking that line are faster than Chuck Yeager.

"Hole number sixteen. Redbud. Might not look like it but this is the easiest par 3 on the golf course. The pin placements are what make a two a tough row to hoe, but there ain't no good reason why you shouldn't make three here ninety percent of the time. Stay away from that top bunker. Unless you're Gary Player, you ain't making three from up there. Green is sloped like a mountain, so when the pin is on the bottom, just throw it into the hill and she'll feed to the hole. The hill is your line when the pin's down at the bottom, anyway. No sense risking that left bunker, forget the pond. Grain is running pretty much dead at us, so putts into the grain here are some of the slowest on the course. What you see is what you get for the yardage, but I ain't gotta tell you that.

"Hole number seventeen. Nandina. See that big ol' loblolly out there in the fairway? That's Ike's Tree. I'm surprised it's still standing, as many times as the old boy hit it. He tried to get Mr. Roberts to cut it down—asked him exactly that during a board meeting. Instead of having to say no to the President of the United States, Mr. Roberts just adjourned the meeting and that was the end of that. Okay, still looking at Ike's Tree, think of your line as being about thirty yards right of it. You can fly it if you want but she's taller than she looks. Not worth it, if you ask me. There's lots of room on the right—you could land a plane over there if you had to. Yardage into the green is a little uphill, adding half a club won't hurt anybody's feelings. Short is a whole lot better than long, and the grain runs hard towards fourteen green. There are some tricky putts on this one. Not just ones breaking up the hill but up a side hill." Freddie tilts his hand at an angle then points to the sky. "Now that's some tricky shit, man.

"Hole number eighteen. Holly. Talk about your great finishing hole. If your man's a player, tell him his line is the clubhouse in the distance. If he can really play, ask him if he sees the three windows that are side by side, under the roofline. If he says yes, tell him to aim at the one in the middle. This is one of the fairways at Augusta you just gotta hit or you'll be scrambling for your par. Right side is death, left side is life support unless you blow it past the bunkers. Opens up a little over there. On your approach shot add a club to whatever the green bible says, and save yourself some heartache by making note of where the pin is when you're making the turn. Nothing kills a tip worse than having your man knock the flag down only to find out it ain't on the back, it's on the front. Or vice versa, which is even worse. This green holds true to memory, so don't forget the grain runs to the big oak below the green, the one between the two fairways. And I mean dead at it. It'll make a straight putt bend the other way every time."

Freddie points down the fairway and angles his hand.

"Last thing. If your man drops it and the member sees him, hand it back and tell him he must have dropped it by accident. You get caught hustling tips and it's a two week vacation. Get caught a second time and you'll be wearing an Aerosmith T-shirt."

"An Aerosmith T-shirt?"

"'Cause your ass is on Permanent Vacation."

31

TUITION TIME

"Hope I didn't short your circuits," says Freddie, dust flying as we pull into the caddy yard. He clicks the brake and I start to get out but he stops me with his hand.

"Be right back," he says.

I look around. A dozen caddy faces are staring me down, no doubt wondering who's the skinny-ass white kid, and he must be somebody special 'cause Freddie don't spend that much time with anybody 'less you about to go to jail. In spite of the magical mystery tour of the world's most revered golf course, I can't help but feel like *I'm* in jail. Minimum security, but jail nonetheless.

Imprisoned by my poor choices.

"Hey, you there. You're Little Doc, ain't ya?"

I look up, face-to-face with a caddy skinny as a pencil lead.

"Sorry," I say. "I didn't—"

"You're Doc's kid. I heard Red call you Little Doc. I've caddied for your daddy lotsa times—especially during Closing Week. He can play a little, your daddy. And can read these greens better than most bulls in the yard."

You don't read these greens, you remember them.

I say nothing, though. I'm just happy to have someone to talk to, even if I have no idea who he is.

"Say, you got two dollars?"

"Two dollars?"

"Yeah. I'm broke. Left with two hundred, came back with two empties. You'll see how it is soon enough."

He points to the pockets of his caddy suit. I reach in mine, pull out two singles from a beat-to-hell wallet, and hand them over.

"You cool if it's tuition?" he asks.

"Tuition?"

"Tuition. Like going to school. Lot cheaper, but you'll learn a lot more. I'm the best teacher in the caddy yard."

I laugh.

He's quick as a cat, back as if he'd never left. He hands me a grape soda in a green Masters cup. A pork chop sandwich is in his other hand, and he bites down on it like he hasn't eaten in days.

"Thanks," I say, even though I'm the one who fronted the dough.

"Thank *you*. Hey, I'm George. But everybody calls me Deal Maker."

"I'm Tripp." I swallow the word *Bowden*. Not sure why.

"I know who you are," he says. "People talk, so what. I just didn't know you knew the Man."

"The Man?"

"Freddie."

"Oh, yeah. He's an old family friend. I've known him since I was a kid."

"Sho nuff?"

"Yeah. Freddie and Doc go way back. Pop's kinda like his doctor, but they're good buds, too."

"Buds?" Deal Maker rolls his fingers, looks at me, and smiles.

"Homies. Brothers." I smile, too. "Kindred spirits."

"I'm all about me some spirits," says Deal Maker.

I laugh, wondering which ones will come back to haunt me.

"Stay away from this one," says Freddie, pointing at Deal Maker. Neither of us heard Freddie's approach. He's light as a bird. Surprising, as big as he is.

"Awww, Freddie. I'm one of the best caddies in the yard. I can teach the kid a thing or two."

"I didn't say you weren't. Didn't say you were, either. Sneakiest. Schemingest. Now *that* I would say."

Deal Maker laughs, and I notice he's backed away from the cart.

It's just a few steps, but to me it's obvious as a canyon. I also notice he didn't take the open seat in Freddie's cart. Not sure if it was out of respect or fear.

I later learn it's both.

"All right, now. I'll be talking to you." Deal Maker shuffles away, a grin on his face like he's up to something. What, I don't know.

I'll find out soon enough.

Freddie hops in the cart, slides two grape sodas into the cup holders, and hands me a pork chop sandwich. I can smell the Texas Pete, and my mouth burns at the thought of it.

We cruise out of the caddy yard, riding in silence, heading in the opposite direction of the golf course. It takes a minute before I realize he's taking me to the parking lot.

Freddie pulls beside my Trans Am and clicks the brake. There's still daylight in the day, but I guess Freddie thinks it's time for me to go.

"How much did he get off you?"

"Who?"

"Deal Maker." The expression on my face answers whatever question he was going to ask next. "See you tomorrow, man. That's enough lessons for one day."

"Hey—how'd you know?"

Freddie drives away, a big grin on his face. "Man, I know everything," he yells, leaving me to the sound of crunching gravel.

32

FIRST STEPS

I wake the next morning before sunrise, beating the alarm clock by half an hour. With unfamiliar hands, I slide on shorts and a golf shirt, slip on my caddy suit, wash the night from my face, and hurry out the door.

Up at sunrise. Check out the new me.

It's weirdly quiet out—too early for school buses or shift workers or anybody with good sense. I have the morning to myself; it belongs to no one else but me.

When I pull through Augusta's main gate and take the required caddy right turn, my private morning disappears. The sun is barely above the trees, chewing the last piece of black from the night, yet the parking lot is almost packed.

Caddies are everywhere.

"Hey, hey. It's Little Doc. Morning to ya."

"Morning," I say, getting out of my car. It's Tip Lite, all bright eyed and bushy tailed.

"Can't let the sun beat you into work, y'know." He beats on his chest like Tarzan.

I'm beginning to see why. Beating the sun, not the chest.

"Who you got today?"

"Who have I got?"

"Who you got? Who you caddying for?"

I shake my head. "Nobody."

"Nobody? Freddie didn't give you no bag yesterday?"

"No. But he rode me around the golf course for a few hours.

Showed me a lot of behind-the-scenes-type stuff, gave me a few tips about the greens. Made me realize I got a lot to learn. I thought I remembered a few things from my college days, but man, was I wrong."

"Shiiiit. You white boys weren't doing nothing but smashing grass." Tip makes horn shapes with his fingers, props them on his head. "Moooooooo. Here come the bulls."

The truth may not set me free, but it definitely makes me laugh.

"Hey, you hungry?"

"I'm always hungry."

"Me and you both," says Tip with a nod like he's trying to convince himself. He pulls a circle of aluminum foil from his pocket and unwraps it. Inside are four sausage biscuits, looking like brown nickels in his massive hands.

"Made 'em fresh this morning," says Tip. "I can cook me some sausage, now. Go on." He pushes his hand to me and I grab one, take a bite. The biscuit is still warm.

He's right. This is damn good.

Tip reaches down and pops a biscuit into his mouth. Three chews and it disappears. He rolls up the foil. "Save these for later. One for me, one for you."

"Thanks," I say.

"Sure," he says. "Come on—let's go get us a bag."

If only it were that simple.

There's a pecking order in the caddy yard, and even though Freddie is the rooster, he knows not to upset a barnyard that took years to perfect. Doctor's son or not, I've got to wait my turn just like everybody else. I'm the only white boy in the caddy yard, though no one seems to notice this but me, and for the first time in my life I'm a minority. But in Freddie's world, there is no black or white. The Marines use the terms light green and dark green. Freddie uses an even simpler term.

Caddy.

The day crawls by as I watch them come and go in a sea of black, white, and green. I kill time by staring at a tiny television, trying to appear interested in a CNN clip about the stock market (I have no money, and certainly no stocks), and then an MC Hammer video. Hammer sings, "You can't touch this," and he's right.

I can't.

For the first time in my life I know what it feels like to be all dressed up with no place to go. I contemplate leaving, contemplate ordering my fifth grape soda of the day. I opt against departure. I don't want to leave Freddie hanging, in case he might need me. I laugh out loud at this. Who the hell would need *me*?

"Tripp!" A voice from behind the wire face of the kitchen booms across the empty room, but I'm too zoned out for it to register. Four caddies walk in, sweaty and complaining about having to go another eighteen.

"I need a beer," one says. "Not no damn soda."

"You and me both," says another.

"I got a cooler in the car," I say, standing up. "Got plenty of cold ones. Coors Light, if that's okay."

"I wouldn't care if it was Miller Lite."

"I wouldn't care if it was a flashlight, long as I could drink it."

"Tripp!" The voice booms again. "Freddie's calling for you. He's got you a bag."

"Who's White Boy got?" A third caddy, the one who mentioned the flashlight, is standing next to me, shoulder to shoulder. He's smiling like he just stole something.

"Tripp got Calamity Jane. Just gonna be him and one of his insurance boys."

"*You* the one gonna need the beer," says the third caddy, popping my shoulder. He turns and offers his hand. "I'm Donahue."

Donahue. The guy who got his ass sliced up by the pampas grass on 7.

"I'm Tripp."

We shake.

"I know who you are."

I surprise myself by pulling the keys from my pocket and handing them over.

"It's the black Trans Am out in the parking lot. Just give my keys to Freddie when you're done."

"No shit?"

"No shit," I say. "Drink one for me."

"He gonna drink more than one," says the first caddy. "Donahue ain't been sober in thirty years."

"Forty," says Donahue, laughing as the five of us walk out into the caddy yard.

They take a left and I take a right. I watch them go, feeling a slight twinge of kinship.

More where that came from, I hope.

* * *

"It ain't much of a bag," says Freddie. "But it beats a blank, and it'll be as good a chance as any to start learning these greens." He picks up the member's bag with one hand, as if the clubs had been removed.

When I throw it over my shoulder I sag under the weight.

"A little advice. Don't give him yardage unless he asks. Don't talk to him unless he speaks to you first. And don't even think about reading the greens for him." He pulls the member's putter out of the bag and hands it over.

"That's a Calamity Jane!" I say, referencing the same type of putter used by legendary Bobby Jones.

Or is it Bob Jones?

Freddie nods. "And the sonofabitch knows how to use it. He's the best putter in the club, hands down. No one's on the same field, much less the ballpark."

"Wow," I say, sliding the putter back in the bag. "Okay—I got it. Carry the bag like a pack mule and don't speak until spoken to."

"Pretend you're a kid from the Victorian age—you don't speak *unless* spoken to." Freddie points out to the practice tee. "They're finishing up lunch. They'll be out there—" he checks his watch— "Ten, fifteen minutes."

I walk to the practice tee and Freddie calls out. "Pay attention, man. To *everything*."

I promise him I will.

33

PAY OUT

"Thanks for putting me out there with Edward," I say. "He's a hell of a caddy."

"One of the best we got," says Freddie. "If not *the* best."

"He really knows his stuff. Didn't even open his yardage book, except to show it to me. Pretty impressive how he's got all the arrows on the greens showing what putt breaks where and why."

"Those are the tricky ones. The ones you thought you remembered but didn't."

"He said he's been here twenty-five years."

"Longer than that," says Freddie, peeling off a twenty, a ten, and a five from a brick-thick stack of bills.

"Cash money," says Freddie. "Uncle Sam ain't getting none of this."

"Cash money," I say, slipping the bills in my wallet. "Thanks."

I'm getting paid what caddies call The Rule: thirty bucks for the Big Course, five for shagging balls. I was caddying for a local, so no dropping it like it's hot. But Freddie's right—it sure beats a blank.

The room grows quiet, the silence oddly welcoming and so we sit there, Caddy Master and caddy. I almost feel like a kid again, like I'm ten years old and Freddie's about to take me fishing. If I close my eyes, I bet I could see that old green cooler overflowing with bream.

"So," says Freddie, breaking the silence. "What do you think?"

"About what?" I ask, still lost in the past.

"About caddying. For real. For a living. Might not be what

you want to be when you grow up, and it won't make you rich, but there ain't no telling who you might meet out here, or where it might lead."

I feel like a line from a Led Zeppelin song.

Yes, there are two paths you can go by, but in the long run,
There's still time to change the road you're on.

"I'll give it a shot," I say, knowing Freddie's right—there really is no telling where this might lead. The stakes get no higher than they do at Augusta National Golf Club.

"You won't regret it," says Freddie. "I promise you that." He snaps two big rubber bands around the thick stack of bills. "Four thousand, three-hundred and eighty-five dollars," he says, sliding the knot into the top drawer.

He doesn't even bother to lock it.

34

CADDY LOGIC

The learning curve in the caddy yard is steep, but when you live on an incline you take any knowledge you can get. With eyes wide open and ears peeled back, I soak in every ounce of knowledge I can.

The months pass quickly, with falling leaves giving way to wintry winds. I take Freddie's advice and never miss a day regardless of conditions, mine or the weather. Winter soon melts into spring, and despite having caddied only six months, I can more than hold my own. I'm also a regular in the caddy house, sitting knee-to-knee with my fellow caddy brothers, eating butter beans for breakfast (I pass on the hot sauce—just simply can't handle it) and drinking grape sodas. I know most of the guys by name: Lamb Chop, Nut, Mack, Bull, Melvin, Po Baby, Hop, Deal Maker, Smitty, Edward, Kimble, Beaver, Bug, First Base, Donahue, Tip.

You name 'em, I know 'em.

Freddie sees to it that I learn from the best, putting me out with elite caddies like Marion and Johnny Bull, Skinny and Smitty, Masters winners all. One of my favorites is Mark, who finished second twice with Johnny Miller. Oddly enough, Mark doesn't have a nickname, although he has one for me: "White Boy." Considering I'm often the only white boy in the caddy yard, especially during slow times, it fits like a favorite pair of shoes.

I don't know how far Mark made it through the educational system—he dropped out of school though I don't know when— but on the greens of Augusta he's a veritable Einstein. He knows these babies like Billy Graham knows the Bible, and he doesn't so much as bend down to read them. God forbid plumb bob. And if he reads one from both sides, the end of the world must be near. Hard as this is to believe, it's not unusual to see Mark read a putt from off the green while raking a bunker, or pulling his player's driver from the bag for the next tee shot.

"It's gonna do what it's gonna do, White Boy," he tells me.

He's right, you know. And that goes for just about anything in life.

It's gonna do what it's gonna do.

35

GUESS WHO'S COMING TO DINNER

"You ain't got a record, do you? And I'm not talking about the kind you put on a Victrola,"

"Huh?" I look at Freddie and shrug.

"A record. A sheet. You ain't fought the law and the law won, have you?"

I'm laughing, now. So is Freddie.

"Speeding ticket's about it. Far as I know."

"Good," says Freddie. "'Cause I need you for a couple of days. Pretty special foursome, this one."

"Sure," I say, wondering who it might be. An athlete? Celebrity? Corporate bigwig? They all come to Augusta to play—to see firsthand what it's like to experience the most private, privileged golf club in the world. To us caddies, it's just grass and sand, but to them it's Nirvana.

"You were handpicked, by the way."

"Really? Wow, thanks."

"Don't thank me. Thank Mr. B."

"Mr. B?"

"Yeah, man. He likes you. So do his guests. That Gannett fellow in particular."

"Wow," I say, wondering where this is leading, but Freddie just leaves it at that. I've already wiped down the clubs, so I slip my guest's bag in the travel carrier, zip it and prop it by the door. At Augusta, very few bags get locked. For every commercial flight there are ten leaving via private plane.

Freddie peels off my day's pay from the familiar stack of bills. Four twenties and a ten.

Not bad. Not bad at all.

"Thanks, Freddie."

"Yeah, man," he says. I get up to leave.

"Democrat or Republican?"

I shake my head. "Neither," I say, letting loose a laugh. "I voted for Ross Perot, if that tells you anything."

"Tells me you ain't no cattle. Tomorrow I want you to be a Republican."

"Sure. But why?"

"'Cause you're caddying in the group with the vice president of the United States."

My mouth opens like a fly trap.

"Dan Quayle?"

"The one and only. Bush wanted to come, but it's too big a hassle. Too much security—and I ain't just talking about the Secret Service. National doesn't want to mess with it anymore. Not after that nut crashed the gate when Reagan was in town."

"I remember that. Held the pro hostage. Wanted to talk to Reagan about his wife leaving him or some such. He was drunk, wasn't he?"

"Stumblin' around the pro shop like a sailor on leave."

I smile. "So I'm caddying for Quayle?"

"No. You're caddying for the guest. He requested you. Mack's caddying for Quayle. He'll be here two days. Thirty-six tomorrow and maybe the Par 3. Eighteen on Thursday, then they fly out in Air Force One."

Freddie says all this as if it's the most natural thing in the world. In his, I suppose it is.

"Mack doesn't have a record?" I ask, half-kidding.

"Not if I can help it," says Freddie.

He's *not* kidding.

36

DAN QUAYLE
AND MOTHER THERESA

I buy a six-pack of tall boys on my way home, crack open the first while sitting on the porch, marveling at my good fortune. After a strong pinch to make sure I'm not dreaming, I tell myself that surely I was chosen because I've become the boss of the moss, the yeoman of yardage, the king of club selection.

Well, that and the fact somebody requested me.

The next morning, after brief, first tee introductions (the VP shakes the hand of every caddy before teeing off, a very cool gesture) and a front nine that flies by like a bottle rocket, it's quite obvious the man who can't spell potato can damn sure spell stripe, dart, and Bobby Locke. Mr. Vice President rips drives straight as a whiskey shot, has missed only two greens out of ten, and rolls the flat stick like he's ready for a Green Jacket. He's burned so many edges I'm surprised he hasn't caught fire.

Make no mistake—Danny Boy can play. If my math is right, he's even par through ten.

I'm standing in the fairway at the crest of the hill on number eleven when the urge suddenly hits. The double transfusion I chugged at the turn—a wonderfully refreshing mix of Welch's grape juice and Canada Dry ginger ale that is a caddy staple—wants out. I look around for a Secret Service Agent, and thankfully see none. I make a beeline for the backside of a loblolly and take care of business fast as I can.

But not fast enough.

Feeling someone's presence, I peer over my shoulder and am suddenly eye to chest with one of the VP's Secret Service agents. He's standing close enough to zip my pants, but I keep my mouth shut and say nothing. He's already been on me twice for going into my pockets at what he felt were inopportune times—to the point of making me empty them out, revealing a half-eaten pork chop sandwich, two chicken legs, and a sausage biscuit wrapped in tinfoil, a good luck gift from Tip Lite.

"You need to eat that . . ."—he so badly wants to say the word "shit"—"*junk* and get it over with." I start chewing like a cow on his cud.

I suppose we all have our moments, moments where we wish life had a *rewind* button, or better yet a *delete* button. Vice President Dan Quayle's moment comes on the 13th at Augusta. After following a balloon of a drive with a perfect layup, Dan's sweet swing turns sour, digging up a beaver pelt big as a lunchbox while sending his Titleist one-hopping into Rae's Creek.

It was as if God had frozen time.

Before anyone can say something, anything—"Too bad, Mr. Vice President," or, "No worries, sir. Just a pitch and a putt and you can save that bogey"—Quayle breaks the silence with a loud reference to "Mother" that isn't followed by "Theresa." Suddenly and wonderfully, the prim and proper, take-that-Murphy-Brown Yale graduate is no longer the vice president of the United States but one of the boys, one of the fellas. Cursing the golf gods for all they were worth.

I'm wrong. This is a *great* golf moment. Hit the *record* button.

If not for the eye daggers thrown at me by the Secret Service gents, I'd walk right over and drape an arm around the VP's shoulder. But the thought of schlepping a fifty-pound golf bag while shackled does not appeal, so I stare at the azaleas and pretend I'm the Pinball Wizard.

You know, that deaf, dumb, and blind kid.

When the round is over, Vice President Quayle announces he has a very special gift for all the caddies. My mind races. Surely not cash money, as tipping is strictly forbidden. But what? A presidential seal on my white jumpsuit?

My jaw drops as the vice president of the United States pulls four white ball caps from a paper bag. The brows of the caps are so high they could pass for John Deere trucking hats if only they were green. But the VP seems awfully proud of them, and he's thanking us like Chip-N-Dale for the great day at Augusta. I fake a smile and pretend to admire the world's ugliest hat.

And then I see it.

Printed on the edge of the cap is the VP's John Hancock. I wet my thumb and give the cap a rub. Nothing. This won't do. A *fake* autograph?

As if reading my mind, the vice president of the United States asks if something is wrong. His eyes are on me, hard as candy.

"Mr. Vice President, sir, could I trouble you for a, uh," I pause, can't believe I'm asking this—"a *real* autograph?"

The VP looks at me and smiles. "Absolutely, Tripp."

The Secret Service agent who had the mezzanine view of my nether region hands Vice President Quayle a Mont Blanc pen. The VP signs my John Deere wannabe hat, hands it back and shakes my hand. He turns to the caddies and says, "Thank you again, all of you, for a wonderful day. And thank *you*, Tripp."

Tripp? As in *me*?

I look down at the hat, admiring the wet ink signature, thinking democracy is a beautiful thing.

37

CLOSING WEEK

Summers in Augusta are sunburns in a steam bath. Augusta National mercifully closes the third week in May, but not without one hell of a sendoff.

Closing Week. Appreciation Week. Six glorious days for a caddy to make as much money as his entrepreneurial instincts will allow. Unlike the regular season, Closing Week knows no similar rules and regulations. Tipping is no longer outlawed, and payment for a job well done comes from the player's pocket, not the Rule Committee.

Freddie gives me a quick lesson on which bags to go after, with each day being different from the last. It's a lot to take in, but I soak it up like a sponge. The summer will be one big blank, as this is the last of the money to be made at Augusta.

"Monday is for the scoreboard folks," says Freddie. "Not a big money day unless you find a Yankee. A straight-up Northern cat. Look for somebody wearing khaki shorts with black socks and Jesus sandals and charge him what you think he'll pay. But make sure you tell him up front, before he takes so much as a practice swing. Keep it at fifty and he'll bite like a stocked-pond catfish.

"Tuesday is gallery guards, the sheriff, police, security, and the folks who run concession. Don't reach for a bag if the owner has a military cut and he ain't military. But if he *is* the real deal, grab his bag like it was made of gold. This day is hit-or-miss, so don't get your hopes up. There's money to be made, but not a lot.

"Wednesday is Vendors Day. Folks like Titleist, Slazenger, Cadillac, and Travelers Insurance, the folks who sponsor the tournament. This is a *big* money day. Just make sure they're wearing something with the Augusta logo, and when they walk up give 'em the best deal you got. Find you a foursome in two carts and think minimum twenty-five a man for the Big Course, ten for the Par 3. Plus tip. Should be a good one.

"Thursday is Media Day. CBS, Chirkinian, the folks who run the local stations. International folks, too. Another good day to make some money, but try to find someone who looks lost, a first-timer. Set your price with him, but don't go beyond a cat eye, and let him tip what he wants.

"Friday's the day you put the gravy on the biscuit. This is Employee Day, and each employee gets to bring a guest, sometimes two, depending on how long they been working for the man. These guests are gunslingers in ways you've never seen. Make sure you get one of these bags. They almost always want to walk, and they always want a caddy. Big money here. You can spot 'em a mile away. Dressing like a tour pro and swinging like a rusty gate.

"Saturday is Employee Day, too. Different day, but same idea. Grounds crew, maintenance. Folks like that. Another big money day 'cause they get to bring guests just like the Friday folks. But be careful who you look for. You want strut and swagger, swagger and strut. Listen for the accent. You want one north of the Mason-Dixon Line. If they show up sounding like your favorite uncle, leave 'em alone.

"Sunday is *your* day, man. Some caddies feel like they got money burning a hole in their pocket and want someone on their bag to return the favor. But I say to hell with that, go play and have fun.

"It's been a long season," says Freddie. "Don't make it any longer by carrying a bag on Caddy Day. If a hundred bucks makes a difference in your life one way or the other, you're in a heap of trouble."

I don't have to look into my wallet to know I'm in a heap of trouble.

38

THE TWIDDLING OF THUMBS

There have been summers of love and boys of summer. The Cars sang of summer, summer, summer, and Billie Holliday sang of summertime, when the living was easy.

This, and I'm not particularly proud to say it, is my summer of doing nothing. Yeah, I play a little golf, an occasional tournament, but I don't grind away like summers past, when visions of a grander stage danced in my head. But to work on my game now would be like remodeling a house you're about to tear down.

What would be the point?

So I spend time working on my novel but the story seems stale, tired to the point that I don't want to write it anymore, much less read it. And if *I* don't want to read it, small chance someone would ever pay for the chance to read it either. So I shelve it, promising to pull it out again when my mind is fresh, the story riveting, the characters full of life and energy.

It is an empty promise.

I wouldn't say I have a pocket full of kryptonite—I don't, although I did manage to save over six grand while walking the Popsicle-green hills of Augusta seven days a week. One of those six is in my wallet now, the others in Ziploc bags under my mattress. A thousand a Ziploc—high denominations, so they lay pretty flat. You would never even know they were there. I know, not the smartest or safest place to keep your money, but no one knows it's there but me and my girlfriend.

My girlfriend, in case I get hit by a bus.

Even doing nothing, my summer flies by. I see Freddie just once, at my folks' house. For reasons I don't remember I'm too busy to talk, my departure as quick as my arrival. I do manage to tell Freddie I'm sorry I can't stay and chat, and that I guess I'll see him in October when the club opens for play.

The look on his face is one I can't decipher. I'm not sure if he's disappointed or appreciative. Not sure which I am, either.

Can't caddy forever, you know. Big world out there, man. Gotta be something out there with your name on it.

I push the thought out of my head and drive away.

39

YOU CAN CALL ME RAY

There's no mention of my return to the caddy yard between Freddie and me, good or bad, and I take it as a sign that it's okay to be back. In the same way a baby won't take his pacifier off to college, I have no plans of being a lifelong caddy.

It is the second week in October, picture day at the caddy house. It's still hot enough to bead sweat on your lip, but at least the days of frying an egg on your sand wedge are gone.

Today is also caddy registration day, where rookies and regulars alike line up to get their picture taken for the yearly ID, get assigned the cherished white jumpsuit, locker number (*if* you are lucky enough—few rookies ever are), FootJoys, green caddy hat, and yardage bible. I'm standing in line with some old teammates from college who are here because Freddie asked me to round up some grass smashers for the days when the National is hopping.

A bunch of us are leaning over the registration table, filling out blue cards that will soon be laminated with our mug shots and become our permanent IDs. There is no entrance through the gates without it. No exceptions whatsoever.

On the card, your given name is typed and there's a blank line for your nickname. *All* caddies have nicknames, from White Boy to Po Baby, Cemetery to Tip Lite. As I'm filling out my card, I glance over and notice that this Pretty Boy Floyd from the golf team—a gent named Forrest who is six feet two and tan as George Hamilton—has neglected to write in a nickname.

I've been caddying long enough to know that this will *never* do. So when Forrest puts his ID card in the stack, I sneak it out and write "Goobah" for his nickname. Southern-speak for Goober, the mechanic from *Gomer Pyle*.

The time comes for Forrest to get his picture taken, and Freddie starts calling out for Goobah. Of course, Forrest has no clue Freddie is calling for him, and there he is standing not three feet away. I casually shrug my shoulders, point to Forrest, and mouth the word "Goobah." Freddie looks at Forrest and says, "Goddamnit, boy! Answer me when I call you. Now get your ass over to the screen so I can take your picture."

Forrest is as lost as a preacher in a porn flick, with a big ol' *What the fuh?* look on his face. Just before he takes the picture, Freddie says, "They named you right, you Goobah-looking mother, you."

It's all I can do not to wet myself from laughing.

Minutes later, Freddie hands Forrest his very own Augusta National Caddy ID and there, in all its laminated glory, is our boy Goobah. Forrest, still terribly confused, looks at the card and says, "Wait, wait. This isn't me. I'm not a Goobah!"

Freddie looks Forrest up and down and says, "Coulda fooled me."

Pretty Boy Floyd never knew who wrote that lovely moniker on his ID, and for the rest of his days as a part-time Augusta National caddy he will be known as Goobah—to the caddies, the pros in the shop, even the players he caddied for.

I'll never forget when one of the pros walked up to Forrest a couple days later, looked at his caddy badge and said: "Goobah? Where the hell did you get a name like *that?*"

I'll never tell.

40

ENGLISH HUMOUR

"A quick eighteen," says Freddie. "Just a threesome, and then they'll be gone. Member's golfed out. He's been here two weeks—thinks he's still in his twenties but he ain't."

A quick glance at my watch reveals it's only five till eight— plenty of time to get out and back. Good chance for an afternoon bag, if I stick around.

But I don't want an afternoon bag. Word in the caddy house is that one of the biggest gunslingers at Augusta is coming in this morning and staying for four days. There'll be big money to be made, as this General Electric CEO pays more than double what most members do.

I stare at the guest's bag like it's a one-year-old with a messy diaper. Not my idea of a good day. His clubs look as old as a Bible verse.

"I need you, man. Wouldn't say it if I didn't."

I don't move as fast as I should—my mind on better money I suppose. I don't realize Freddie's gone until I hear his office door bang shut.

I grab the bag and walk to the driving range. I'm not ten feet in the parking lot when its owner stops me. "No practice for me, mate. I'm too far gone for that."

I turn to the voice. Standing before me is a nattily dressed Englishman, offering his hand. He's sporting a Ben Hogan–style cap and a shit-eating grin.

I like him immediately.

Freddie was right. These boys mean business, giving new meaning to the term "hit it and get it." There's no cake in their walk, a gimme has no predetermined length, and a ball off the beaten path—left of 2, right of 5—is deemed lost forever. Small matter, since no one is keeping a cumulative score. They're playing match play, where each hole is a new beginning.

"Who gives a damn about my eight on number two? It beats the shit out of your nine!"

My kind of golf.

We stop at the halfway house, which at Augusta is a simple green cart with even simpler fare. Crackers and candy bars. Soft drinks and beer. A liquor drink should the urge hit. But if you want a hot dog or a sandwich, it better already be in your bag.

"Pity they don't let you chaps have a taste," says the Englishman, making short work of his vodka tonic. "You certainly earn it, walking these God-awful hills in those thick jumpsuits. I get hot just looking at them." He slams back his drink. "And the way you lads read these greens. I was telling my caddy yesterday I don't even bother to look anymore. Just line me up and I'll knock them down."

There's a big laugh from his playing partners. I get the joke. The Englishman hasn't made a putt longer than his shoe all day.

He swaps his empty cup for a driver and we make our way to 10.

I wish all bags were like this, I think to myself as we litter Augusta's back nine with pars and bogeys. The Englishman couldn't care less if they're eagles or triples. He is the rarest of Augusta National guests. Far from obsessed with kissing up to the member, or the numbers on the scorecard, this guy's just happy to be here.

"So," he says, as we wait for his playing partners to hit their approach shots, "What in bloody hell are *you* doing out here?"

Thinking it's just more of his English humor, I shrug up my shoulders and smile.

"Seriously, friend. You don't fit the Augusta caddy mold. And I don't mean just because you're white."

A long pause.

"Don't know," I say. And it's true, I don't.

"You're bright, educated, witty—just like me." He nudges my shoulder with a gentle fist. "This just doesn't seem like your, shall we say, permanent cup of tea."

The smile disappears.

"Please, don't get me wrong," says the Englishman. "You're an excellent caddy. Especially for only being out here a year."

His comment takes me by surprise. "How'd you know that?"

"The Caddy Master—that Freddie gentleman. He assured me I was in very capable hands this morning when it became obvious my man had taken a sabbatical. My fault for tipping before the last day, I suppose."

My eyes lift up at the T-word.

"So, 9-iron or wedge?" he asks.

"Wedge," I say, eager to earn that tip. "Your adrenaline is pumping. A 9-iron would still be climbing as it took pictures of the flag."

"When my adrenaline pumps, I promise you it is not on any golf course," he says, laughing.

I'm not sure you'd say I earned that tip, but I got it anyway. After putting out on the 14th green and giving his playing partners ample time to put space between us, the Englishman unzips his bag and drops in a twenty, what we caddies call a dub, the crisp bill neatly folded.

"Thank you," he says, patting my shoulder.

"Thank *you*," I say, slipping the bill into my coveralls.

I should thank him a lot more. I don't know it at the time, but that Englishman is my ticket out of here.

41

THE SMOKING SECTION

"Guess what this cat owns," says Freddie, pushing a bag in my direction. I flip over the name tag. No bells ring.

"Pebble Beach."

"This guy *owns* Pebble Beach? As in the golf course?!"

"Resort, too," says Freddie. "I'm telling you, man, the Japanese yen is stronger than Skinny's drawers. It's cheaper for them to hop a flight to California for the weekend than it is to play eighteen at the local country club."

"That's crazy."

"Yeah, but the whole world's crazy, so it makes perfect sense to me." Freddie takes his finger and wipes a smudge of dirt off the 7-iron. "This one's easy money, if you know how to do the do."

"I do indeed," I say.

Freddie smiles. "Those Japanese folks pay out like a slot machine. Monopoly money is all it is to them. They pass Go in their sleep."

I grab the bag and sling it over my shoulder. Freddie points to the 1st tee.

"Straight to the box, man. They don't care anything about warming up."

"Works for me," I say.

After brief introductions, my player (he tells me to call him Bob, of all things) wastes little time and stripes one down the middle about 220 yards out. His playing partners say quiet words and bow, broad smiles across their faces. The member seems miles away, his mind on a business deal, I'm guessing.

After a routine par and another fairway splitter on the 2nd, Bob stops me at the top of the hill, waiting for the others to pass. I can see he's guarding his pockets, and he's shifting side to side like he's standing on a bed of smoldering charcoal. He leans in to whisper.

"Can you smoke—at Augusta?"

I stare at the ground, as if this question requires deep thought. What an odd thing to ask, but Freddie has taught me well. Any angle is a good angle for angling a tip. "You can *today*," I say. "Just be discreet about it." I slide a finger over my lips and nod.

Bob slides a pack of Dunhills from his pocket, slips one in his mouth, and lights it with a gold Zippo. It's monogrammed, and I can't believe what it says.

Bob.

He takes a deep drag and brings the cigarette behind his back, cupping it from view.

"Perfect," I say, patting Bob on the shoulder. He thanks me with a hundred-dollar bill so crisp you'd swear he printed it on the flight over.

It's a quick loop, less than three hours, and Bob and I yuk it up with caddy-speak and broken English. I deal him most of my aces— the water fountain on 5 (he laughs like a kookaburra when he tells his friends as they walk up the hill, their mouths dry as dust), the Indian burial ground on 12. He oohs and ahhs like a little kid.

After the round, Bob stops me before I can walk off the green. The member is long gone, having picked up his ball after three karate chops from the bunker.

"Thank you, Mr. Tripp, for a most wonderful day."

"My pleasure," I say, and it certainly is.

"Pebble Beach for you, anytime. Just tell them Bob say: okay *anytime*." He bows before offering his hand. I shake it. There's no money, but I can't help but think this handshake is something even better.

Appreciation.

When I walk into Freddie's office he looks up from his little black book, where the names of every caddy who's walked these hills and every member who's swung his sticks are neatly written in pencil. I guess the look on my face is what's keeping him quiet, so I walk over to his desk and unfold my hand.

The cat eye drifts down and Freddie smiles.

42

MOVERS AND SHAKERS

It's hard to fathom the sort of people who play Augusta National on a regular basis. Sure, the guest list is impressive, but not nearly as impressive as the membership. Celebrities are one thing, but they don't shape the economy, and they damn sure don't have the power to change the world.

These men do.

Augusta National counts the CEOs of General Electric, Chevron, AT&T, and Coca-Cola among its impressive list of members. And I'm not including two of the three richest men in the world.

You know who they are.

I've seen them come and go on a regular basis for over a year now, and it's still hard for me to believe. But to Freddie, they're just people, no different than you or me. They just put on a hundred-dollar tie when they go to work instead of a caddy suit.

"They put their pants on one leg at a time, same as the rest of us," says Freddie.

Maybe that's why they like him so much. I watch it from a distance, sometimes observe it up close. Freddie gives them service, absolutely the best in the business. But he doesn't kiss ass, never treats them like anything but who they really are. Men. People. Human beings. Folks.

Folks. That's the word that fits them best.

Just plain folks who shed their skin when they drive down Magnolia Lane and into the protective arms of the most exclusive golf club in the world.

I'm caddying for one of these folks today. Plain, yes, but he also happens to be the founder of one of the world's largest tabloids.

People magazine.

For once Freddie doesn't give me any background on my player, and it's not until the back nine that I realize who I'm caddying for. It's one of those "No shit?" moments in life when you know what you heard and you know you heard it right. You just simply can't believe it.

"*Really*?" I say. "You founded *People* magazine?"

"Yep," he says. "That would be me."

He's almost blushing.

I give him the yardage, though the distance to the flag is the furthest thing from my mind. I feel I have to ask him something, anything. How often do you find yourself in such company?

I jump in headfirst, random thoughts flying.

"Where'd you get the idea?"

He turns to face me.

"What idea?"

"*People* magazine," I say, handing him his putter, forgetting—at least for the moment—this man is playing Augusta National and his mind is miles away from anything else.

"Oh, that," he says, as if he's talking about a scratch on his elbow, but there's a smile on his face. "It just came to me one afternoon. One of those things that seems so obvious, so part of everyday life, you don't see it for the great idea that it is. That's why so few people ever have them." He shakes his head. "I shouldn't say that. Almost everybody has these ideas. But not everybody *recognizes* them, much less acts on them. For every FedEx there's a million people sitting behind a desk, pushing paper and wishing they had thought of it first, when in fact they probably had."

My wheels, usually spinning at a time like this, are instead turning.

"I read somewhere," I say, not sure where exactly, "that FedEx was born from a term paper. And the guy who wrote it didn't even make an A."

"Yep," he says. "Got a C-plus. Professor didn't think it would fly. Ten thousand jets and enough white trucks to populate the country later, I'd say he was wrong. You know, Mr. FedEx is a friend of mine. Our wives grew up together."

"Really?"

"No," he says, laughing. "Just seeing if you were paying attention."

I want to shout, "I am!" but instead I just nod like a bobbing doll on a road full of potholes.

"So, my putt," he says. "Any thoughts on a read?"

It's obvious I haven't been paying attention.

"Three balls on the left," I say, hoping I'm at least in the ballpark. "And it's fast. You're running with the grain."

"Where's the fun in that?" he says, smiling. "I'd rather go against it."

Been doing that his whole life, I'll bet.

He two-putts for his par, and as we walk to the next tee I have to ask him. My Nan would flatten my biscuits if she knew I was caddying for the founder of her favorite tabloid and didn't even mention her name.

"My grandmother absolutely *loves* your magazine," I say. "It's the only Christmas present she ever asks for. Well, that and jewelry."

"Thanks," he says, snapping his fingers. "That reminds me. I didn't answer your question—you asked me where I got the idea for the magazine." He reaches into his bag and pulls out an 8-iron. "I may sound like a simpleton, but the idea behind *People* is as basic as human nature. Very few of us will ever be famous, but we are all intrigued and attracted to those who are. That's what I call the celebrity factor. But bigger than that is this simple truth. There's not a soul out there that doesn't want to read about, doesn't care to know about people who are better off and people who are worse."

I hand him his 6-iron, put the 8 back in the bag. I doubt he came all the way from New York to lay up on the 12th at Augusta. I tell him his line is the green strip of grass between the two back bunkers.

"Think about that," he says. "No matter the situation, there is *always* going to be somebody better off than you, and *always* somebody worse."

"Life in a nutshell," I say.

"Life in a nutshell," he repeats.

I lean the bag on the bench, hoping he remembers his line.

I know I will never forget it.

43

I'M IN THE JAILHOUSE NOW

I'm biting into my first pork chop sandwich of the day, grease dripping down my fingers. But it's good grease, a staple of the caddy life. I know orange juice isn't just for breakfast anymore, and the fact that pork chops have taken their place suits just fine. I put a grape soda to my lips, and I see him over the rim.

"Beaver," I say, surprised to see one of Augusta's finest at this ungodly hour. He's been gone for a week, maybe two. "Where you been, man?"

Beaver is one of the top caddies at Augusta and has been walking these fairways since Kennedy raised his right hand. He's assertive, in his own unique way. He's also crazy as a shithouse rat. Maybe that's why I like him so much. I got some shithouse rat in me, too.

"Where you think I been, White Boy?"

I shrug my shoulders. I have no idea.

"Been where I always go when I do wrong."

"That doesn't really narrow it down," I say, laughing. Beaver likes me, so I know I can get away with saying it.

"Jail, man. Jay-hey-hey-ail. Just call me Elvis. Jailhouse rock."

"What'd you do?"

"It's what I didn't do."

"What *didn't* you do?"

"Pay child support, but I ain't even sure it's my kid. But my vote don't count in the system. That's just the way it is, White Boy. Black, white, green. Don't matter. Gonna get you too, one day, if you ain't careful. I 'magine you know that, smart as you is."

I don't, I want to say, but I sit still as a possum and say nothing.

"Freddie got me out," says Beaver, as if that's the answer to my next question.

"Freddie?"

"Yeah, my main man's in town all week. He sends me money in the summer, when the golf course closes and I ain't got a nickel in my pocket. Can't miss out on *him*. No, sir."

"Freddie bailed you out of jail?"

"Damn straight. Freddie bail us all out. And not just outta jail."

"Wow," I say. "I had no idea Freddie was a bondsman."

"Best in town," says Beaver, motioning to the fry cook for a bone sandwich.

"Gimme two, Roundhead! They don't feed you for shit in the jailhouse."

"Gimme" is the operative word. Beaver's pockets are as empty as a summertime school bus.

"You know one of the best things about it?" says Beaver, attacking the sandwich.

"About what? Jail?" I shake my head. Nothing could be good about that.

"Freddie don't want no up front money. Sometimes he don't want *any* money. And sometimes he just garnish your wages. A twenty here, a ten there. Freddie don't ever break you. That's one of the things I like about that man." Beaver sucks down his grape soda, not bothering to come up for air. He brings it down and rattles the ice. "Roundhead, can I get me a refill? Got a mouth full of cotton over here!"

It's hard to tell who he's addressing, because he's looking dead at me.

"He do it for you, too," says Beaver. "And not just 'cause you're Doc's boy. Uh-uh." Beaver points at me with his sandwich, what little there is left of it.

"He do it for you 'cause you one of us. You a caddy. And a pretty damn good one." He looks at me as if sizing me up. "Never thought I'd see it—a white boy knowing this place like us." Beaver takes a big bite of the second bone sandwich and stuffs it into his jumpsuit, not bothering to wrap it up.

"Thanks," I say, and I mean it. This is pretty high praise coming from one of the best caddies at Augusta National.

"Yeah, you pretty good—for a *white boy*," says Beaver. He pops me on the shoulder, laughing as he walks out the door.

44

BRIC-A-BRAC

"Name's Bric-a-Brac."

"Bric-a-Brac?"

"Yeah. Don't ask me where it came from. Damn if I know."

He offers a hand and we shake. No stilted, white-boy, Corporate-America shake. There are fingers, palms, fists, and motion. The handshake of brothers, no matter what blood flows through our veins.

Bric's a caddy. By definition, he is my brother.

"Who you got? The member?"

I shake my head. "Cat from California. A guest. Freddie says he owns a winery."

"Oooo-weee. Drop it like it's hot."

"Hope so," I say.

"Know so," says Bric.

It's a quick eighteen, with the Par 3 course a series of beaver pelts and pickups. But this member pays big, and when we stand at the pay window Freddie doles out eighty bucks a man for four hours' work.

There is still plenty of sun in the sky, but our workday is done.

Bric fans the bills. "Let's go enjoy this. My treat. You kick in what you got when it's gone."

I stare at my eighty bucks, very tempted to say *why not?*

"Bric," yells Freddie, pushing open his office door. "Go tell Roundhead I need to get a new pair of shoes for Donahue. His main man is coming this afternoon and Donahue ain't got so much as socks on his feet."

This doesn't sit so well with Bric.

"Can't you just call him?"

"Damn intercom ain't working. Now go on," Freddie pauses, "*if* you want to get paid."

Bric takes off like he was shot out of a cannon.

For the first time in my life, Freddie is angry and in my face.

"Don't even think about it. I don't care if he's promising you a rose garden. Bric's a good guy in a bad way. Nothing but headache and heartache coming out of him."

Freddie looks down at the caddy house. "That crack ain't no monkey on your back, man. It's goddamn Willie B!"

Willie B is the personable gorilla at the Atlanta Zoo who is as loveable as Christmas but can also be mean as a snake. I start to laugh at the analogy, but the expression on Freddie's face stops me cold.

When Bric comes back, I tell him I can't go.

"Sorry Bric. Got too much stuff to do. Miles to go before I sleep."

It's a bad joke, but Bric gets it. He also busts it.

"Miles to go before you talk a bunch of shit, White Boy," says Bric, a crazy smile on his face as he slaps me on the chest and walks out the door. "That's all right, White Boy. I'm cool with it." He throws Freddie a stare. "See ya tomorrow."

"See you, Bric," I say.

Freddie says nothing.

Tomorrow never comes.

When Bric leaves the golf course, he heads straight to a crack house, one I know but never frequent except to drop off a random caddy. I am not one to judge, have never been one to judge. Back in the wild days I smoked my share of weed, until a joint laced with angel dust cured me for life. But weed ain't crack. Not even close.

Bric's night got long and his night got ugly. The sun came up to witness Bric-a-Brac pulling a gun on his fiancée, a nurse with a good job and hopes and dreams just like he once had. Angry words fly before Bric shoots her point blank in the face, ending the conversation and, moments later, her life.

I come to work the next morning, not an hour removed from the tragedy. There will be no need for Freddie to say I told you so.

He already has.

45

BREAKFAST AT TIFFANY'S

"What'cha doing for lunch, man?"

I weigh my options like a broken Scales of Justice. Pork chop sandwich, chicken sandwich, pack of Nip Chee crackers, and a grape soda. It's a rare day when there's a break in the action long enough to warrant a trip to the Chick-Fil-A.

"Wide open," I say.

"Got some shrimp fried rice," says Freddie. "From Peking."

My mouth waters, and not just at the menu item. From the Augusta National to the Augusta Water Works, everybody knows Freddie. If Freddie called in the order, shrimp fried rice from Peking means they'll be jumping out the box.

I pull up the chair next to his desk and sit down.

"The member I set you up with—he ain't all bad, is he?"

I shake my head. "He's a different sort of duck, but you can tell he's a good guy deep down."

"'Bout half crazy, but ain't we all?" says Freddie with a smile. "He asked for you, in a roundabout way. You caddied for one of his guests. That English cat. Remember? The bag you didn't want?"

"Oh, yeah," I say, a little embarrassed. I don't mention the permanent-cup-of-tea inquiry. "Dropped a twenty on me coming off fourteen green. He was good stuff, even without the tip."

"He thought you were, too," says Freddie. "He told Gumby as much. So when the Englishman ain't here, you are now officially Gumby's main caddy."

"That's awesome," I say. "Thanks, Freddie."

I chew a shrimp and smile. Gumby is a good bag to have. The rare member who comes for two weeks at a time during the slow months, the cold months, the lucky-to-get-out-there-at-all months.

This isn't pennies from heaven—this is silver dollars.

"That Englishman is a big-time advertising guy—a CEO, I think. A Madison Avenue man. Runs the show—the whole kit and caboodle. Might want to bend his ear next time he's down. He and Gumby are pretty close. Comes down at least twice a year, sometimes three or four."

"I'm on it," I say, with a shrimp in my mouth. I know what's coming next, and in spite of the new opportunity and the unknown possibilities from Gumby and the Englishman, I'm dreading it.

The question I have no answer for.

What'cha gonna to do with your life, man? Can't caddy forever, you know.

Trust me, I know.

46

SAME OLD LANG SYNE

It's two days before Christmas and Augusta National is a ghost town. I'm here only because I have nowhere else to go. There are no bags to be had, only conversation to be heard. But today will be the best gift I'll get this year. Freddie, holding court.

It's just me and three other regulars, guys who are here no matter what. Rain, sleet, snow. Hurricane or holiday.

Freddie pops the top on a Coke as I walk in.

"No, he didn't!" yells one of the regulars. "Dropped dead walking up number five?"

I grab a chair and slide up to Freddie's desk.

"What?" I say. "Somebody just died?"

"As sure as I'm sitting here," says Freddie, but not to me. "He was playing in a onesome, trying to get in one last eighteen before the club closed for the summer." Freddie shakes his head and points a finger to the ground. "Poor sonofabitch was dead before he hit the grass."

The room grows quiet.

"Now, that crazy-ass caddy," says Freddie, twirling a pen. "He takes off the dead man's watch, pulls out the money bag, and hops his black ass over the fence and hightails it down Berckmans Road. Not even thinking about his car in the parking lot. And him with a sheet a mile long."

We shake our collective heads. I've done some crazy things in my life, but taking money off a dead man is not one of them.

"I call White Horse Package soon as I hear what happened. I knew that was the first stop for that crazy old coot. Five grand will buy a lot of Ripple."

There's lots of laughter, but I still don't know the joke.

"So I catch his ass as he's walking out the White Horse, loaded down with booze and cigars. Musta had fifty of 'em bulging out his caddy suit. We don't even speak. Don't need to. I just motion him into the car. Thank God his dumb ass had the sense enough to get in. He goes to the Big House this time, he ain't coming out unless he's in a box."

"You too much, Freddie," says a regular, laughing and slapping Freddie's desk.

"So I bring him back here, tell him to empty out his pockets. Tell him I'll pay him for nine holes, even though they only made four and a half. I don't think the old man will mind. No use for it where he's going."

Freddie takes a sip of Coke and lights a Malboro. "Seen a lot of things in my day, but I ain't *never* seen no hearse with a luggage rack."

We're all laughing now.

"That ain't the end of the story," says Freddie as the laughter dies down. He leans in and so do we, as choreographed as a Broadway musical.

"While crazy-ass Charlie is emptying out his pockets he looks at me serious as can be and says, 'Awwww, c'mon, Freddie. You know he woulda wanted me to have that money.'"

"I pull up the sleeve on his caddy suit and say: 'The Rolex, *too?*'"

Everyone busts out laughing.

"Crazy-ass caddy," says Freddie, tossing his empty Coke can into the trash.

No one leaves the room. We just sit there grinning, waiting for the next yarn to be spun.

47

THE BANK OF FREDDIE

There's nothing like watching Freddie in action. Like Hamlet, there's a method to his madness, a reason for everything he does. The reasons might not always be in the so-called rule book of life, but they're always the *right* reasons.

Few people would believe what Freddie does for others, caddies in particular, especially if all they see is the ass-chewing he gives them (myself included) when the situation warrants. But Freddie never raises his voice unless the situation calls for it. I wouldn't say he does it because he feels wronged or taken advantage of. No, I'd say he does it because he's disappointed. Few people believe there is as much good in the world as Freddie Bennett.

Not everyone sees this side of him, and Freddie doesn't show it to just anyone. I've been witness to it half my life and yet today is a surprise, even for me.

It's a Sunday afternoon in April. The golf course is packed like a Who concert, with much money to be made from all the gunslingers in town. It's not unusual for a caddy to pocket $250 or more on days like this.

Speaking of—

I know what I'm seeing but it doesn't quite register—like something that flies onto your radar, only to become a blip on the screen. I don't think too much of it at first, the random caddy walking up to Freddie and quietly slipping him a Jackson, a McGarrett, a Cat Eye. But then it sticks in my head like a migraine.

It's way too early for football and nobody bets on baseball.

And no way is Freddie on the take.

I stop a caddy who just slipped Freddie a stack of twenties. I stop him only because I know him. He's one of my boys.

"Donahue," I say. "Did you just give Freddie—money?"

"Yep. He keeps it for me. Keeps it for a lot of the guys. The First National Bank of Freddie." Donahue laughs. "Better him than those goats."

By goats he means women. Goats like paper, and paper is caddy-speak for money.

"Get out," I say. "Freddie holds your money?"

"You damn right. Most guys out here don't trust banks, and even if we did we ain't got a car to get us there. This way we know where it is. All we gotta do is come to work and get it. Freddie's been my bank for over twenty years. That bank ain't never been robbed, ain't never lost money. Why would I go anywhere else?"

Donahue puts a hand on my shoulder and smiles.

The Bank of Freddie is on my radar for the rest of the season. A steady stream of customers will frequent the establishment, some more often than others. At season's end, the bank closes and the deposits are returned. Not one customer ever counts his money.

That's how much they trust the banker.

48

ME AND THE MVP

The sun and moon have yet to swap places, but that doesn't keep my phone from ringing. To my surprise, I answer it. Freddie's voice is on the other end, barely above a whisper.

"You need to see this."

"What?" My voice is like gravel, a train derailed.

"You need to see this."

I nod as if he can see me, tell him I'm on my way. I don't remember if I brush my teeth or comb my hair. It's all I can do to find my caddy hat.

Berckmans Road is deserted, and I'm through the gate in less than five minutes. There are only a couple of cars in the parking lot, so I slip the Trans Am up front. There are no lines defining spaces, just grass and gravel. The rocks crunch under my feet and I start waking up, hurrying best I can.

The only lights are security lights and the little yellow bulb above Freddie's office door. Freddie's standing there, arms spread wide in the frame, looking as if he never left. He says nothing, just points to the putting green. I walk around the corner, stopping at the Bobby Jones sundial.

There's a man on the green, rolling putts as the sun slowly climbs the sky behind him. But I don't need sunlight to know who it is.

Michael Jordan, of the world champion Chicago Bulls. The reigning MVP. I wonder if he's wearing his ring. It would be his third, I think.

There's a certain aura to Jordan, and I can feel it even from here. I know I shouldn't stare, but I can't help it.

Jordan looks up, gives a quick nod, and smiles. I smile back. Just player and caddy acknowledging one another, not rabid hoops fan fawning over the biggest name in sports. He rolls in another putt and I think—not for the first time—that Augusta National is as much a haven as it is a golf course.

Freddie was right.

I needed to see this.

49

BENEDICT ARNOLD

With my second season and Caddy Day just a sunset from being in the books, I drive the cart over to the 10th tee, eager for one last nine. I never know when the pro is going to blow the whistle, but if it's anytime soon I'd rather it be back here.

Speak of the devil.

Before I can put a tee in the ground, the pro pulls up and lowers the boom. It falls like an imploded skyscraper.

"That's it, boys. Caddy Day is officially over. All caddies have got to go. Time to vacate the premises."

"Aww, man. There's like three hours of daylight left."

"Orders from the top," says the pro. "Don't shoot me, Gator. I'm just the messenger."

"But why?" I ask. "We bust our ass all year long for the chance to play. What's another few hours? It's not like we're in somebody's way."

The pro shrugs his shoulders. "Grounds crew wants to do a few things to the golf course. They can't do it with caddies running all over the place."

"Do a few things to the golf course? They've got the next *five months* to do a few things to the golf course."

"Sorry, Gator. Like I said, not my rules."

The other caddies in my group slump back to their carts and drive away, cursing under their breath. Donahue, my caddy for the day, takes a finishing sip of his Miller Lite.

"Don't matter," he says, crushing the green wax cup against his knee. "We're outta beer anyway."

I start to press the pedal, but the pro shakes his head.

"Not you, Tripp. Just the caddies. *You* can stay."

Donahue looks at me with an expression I'll never forget. He probably never forgot mine, either. I pull a cat eye from my wallet and slip it to him as he exits the golf cart.

"Ain't no thang, Boss. Not like it ain't never happened before." Donahue opens his hand, sees the cat eye and smiles, a banana of a grin. "You a damn good man, Tripp Bowden. Anybody ever told you that?"

"You a damn good caddy, Roger Donahue. Anybody ever told *you* that?"

His face lights up. "Just now." He slides the cat eye into his pocket and walks away. I guess he knows I'm watching, because he waves goodbye without turning around.

I should walk away with him, but I don't. Instead, I drive my cart to the 1st tee, where my dad and the pro are waiting.

Not you, Tripp. Just the caddies. You can stay.

Damnit, I'm a caddy too!

"I can't do it," I say to Pop. "It's not right." I turn the cart around and tell Donahue to hop in. Together we head for the parking lot.

That's what I should have done, but I didn't.

I regret it to this day.

50

A SUMMER OF CHANGE

I'm sitting beside Freddie's desk with season two officially in my rearview mirror. The guilt from staying to play when all my caddy brothers were forced to leave is slowly drowning in my tenth beer of the day. Or is it my twelfth?

Freddie is sitting behind his desk, organizing the drawers like a player might do to his locker after a game. But Freddie's season never ends at Augusta. He'll be here tomorrow just like today, even though some days there's no one here but him.

"So, you got the job?"

"I got the job," I say, raising my beer.

Truth be known, I pretty much created it. But there was a void to be filled so I filled it. Kind of like rain following clouds.

"That's great," says Freddie, his eyes staring down into the confines of his desk drawer.

I feel like shit, feel like I should get up and leave, give Freddie privacy, but I'm waiting on Pop and I have nowhere to go but the parking lot.

I also don't really want to leave.

It's suddenly quiet, so quiet. I break the silence with the only hammer I've got.

"Thanks again, Freddie. It's been a great year."

"Yeah, man," he says, his mind somewhere else. Pop knocks on the door but doesn't come in. He points to his car, a white Karmann Ghia that has made many a trip down Magnolia Lane.

I leave without saying goodbye. Why should I?

I know I'm coming back.

51

CUTHBERT

I spend the summer of '91 in the Deep South, in a town with no stop light. Cuthbert, Georgia, where Mom grew up and her mother still lives. She's eighty-four, my grandmother, still a nurse at the local hospital, and can lay an honest claim to delivering almost every person in town. Some of the deliveries were famous, like football star Rosie Grier and former heavyweight champion of the world Larry Holmes. Holmes even gave my grandmother an autographed photo from the night he won his first belt, gloves raised and him snarling like something just bit him on the ass and wouldn't let go. She gave it to me one Christmas, and it hasn't been seen since.

Instead of the Augusta National Golf Club and a caddy house to call home, my summer office will be Randolph Country Club, a little nine-hole track with postage-stamp greens and fairways harder than a Rubik's Cube. You may remember it. It's where I broke 50 to earn my first pair of golf shoes.

I still have those shoes. White FootJoys with mud flaps over the laces, the spikes caked with red Georgia clay.

Man, has this place changed.

Gone are head pro Tom Lacey and his cronies who loved to play six-somes, each man in his own cart so you can eat up as much daylight as possible. I'm told Tom had gotten too old, too feeble, and is biding his time in an assisted-living home in Albany.

That's a shame. Tom was a great man.

I look around the pro shop, and all I see are a few boxes of shoes, stacks of Nip Chee crackers, and a hot dog steamer. I'm sure there's a cash register, but for the life of me I can't find it. (I later learn Randolph Country Club is an honor system, and a cigar box doubles as the cash register.)

You make your own change here, just like you do in life.

I rub my hand across a box of Dexters, thinking how nice it was to finally have an answer to Freddie's favorite question.

"What'cha gonna do with your life, man? Can't caddy forever, you know."

I do know, and for the first time I have an answer.

"I'm teaching golf," I say. "Starting a junior golf program at a club in south Georgia that never had one before."

"Giving back to the community," says Freddie. "That's always a good thing."

Who cares if it's only for ninety days?

Staring at my watch, wondering where are all the kids who saw the ad in the paper and begged and pleaded, pleaded and begged their moms and dads to pay the forty bucks a week for a crash course in golf, I can't help but feel a little like the guy in the Buffett song.

It's my job, to be cleaning up this mess, and that's enough reason to go for me.

It's my job, to be better than the rest, and that makes the day for me.

It *is* my job. And I plan on doing it right.

I push open the metal door and walk outside. It's only nine o'clock, but the sun is pounding down on me like a schoolyard bully. I make my way to the practice green to roll a few putts, and just like that I'm a kid again. Twelve years old and clueless. Freddie's voice is in my ear.

If you can't putt, you can't play.

Suddenly, the sound of wheels on gravel, slamming doors, and high-pitched voices. The faces that look at me quickly look away. With my surfer-dude hair and John Daly Pump Reeboks, I look more like a lifeguard than a golf pro.

It hits me. I'm not a pro.

Something else hits me, too. Who gives a damn? Thanks to Freddie, I learned the game the right way. Fundamentals and rules.

Rules and fundamentals. Learn 'em all, then bend 'em however you see fit.

If you can't putt, you can't play.

By the time August is over, you'll say these kids can play.

52

LIGHTENING THE MOOD

Season three rolls in like a creature of habit, and once again I don the white suit. I had hoped to teach golf into the fall, but when school started the pool of kids eager to learn the great game of golf dried up like a mud puddle. There are no life questions from Freddie and for this I am glad. I tell myself that the simple fact I tried something, anything, was enough.

I have only two seasons under my belt, but I've been standing on the shoulders of giants and am considered one of the better Augusta caddies. I'm no Carl Jackson, no Edward, no Mark, Bull, or Melvin. But I am a far, far cry from a grass smasher.

I caddy every day—no days off—and the money rolls in. Not hand over fist, but footstep over footstep. This works just fine for me.

I'm between rounds, sitting beside Freddie's desk, watching time creep by on slow legs. I don't notice the four-pack of lightbulbs sitting on the desk until Freddie picks the box up, as if to examine it. He pulls a Sharpie from his pocket, pops off the top and writes. When he puts the box back on the desk he spins it around.

I recognize the caddy's name. In fact, I know him well.

Freddie throws me a look that I can't quite figure out and pushes the lightbulbs closer to the front edge of his desk. I don't know whether to laugh or be serious as a funeral.

But I *have* to ask.

"What's up with the lightbulbs?"

Freddie brings his hands together. "Ol' Theo. You know he's been gone from here over a month now. Couldn't pay his woman so they made him pay the man."

I guess the look on my face is one of confusion because he points to the box of bulbs.

"Behind on child support. That sonofabitch has kids scattered all over town. Like he doesn't know what causes 'em to get here. Long and the short, all the women got together and turned him in. Lucky he didn't get a year. Somebody must have bailed him out."

I can guess who.

"Crazy," I say. "How many kids does he have?"

"How many fingers you got?"

"Theo has *ten* kids?"

"At least," says Freddie. "And he's married, too. Or was until last night."

"Last night?"

"When Theo got home from the Big House—his place, he bought it—he walked in and flipped on the lights, but no lights came on. And not because the electricity had been cut off. No, sir. The old lady, she'd taken everything. The TV, refrigerator, furniture. Everything. Even the damn lightbulbs!"

I don't mean to laugh but I do.

When Theo comes off the golf course, he walks into Freddie's office to get paid and picks up the box with his name written on the side.

"What's up with the lightbulbs, Freddie?"

"You said your old lady took everything. Well, these won't get you back on your feet but at least you'll be able to see the sonofabitches!"

Theo, no stranger to settling his disputes with a gun, laughs until his stomach hurts.

"You all right, Freddie Bennet," says Theo. "You all right."

53

REALITY BITES (BUT NOT THAT HARD)

"You hungry?"

"I'm always hungry."

Freddie slides over a heaping bowl of clam chowder.

"Chef Clark's secret recipe, man."

I know the recipe well. It's Campbell's soup, Borden's half and half, and a handful of minced clams thrown in for good measure. Just like the regaled tilapia recipe, the members of Augusta wouldn't believe this one either.

Lunches with Freddie. I cherish every one of them.

Outside the air is cold, skin-tingling, and biting. Only eight players are on the grounds today, but one of them is mine. Augusta is pretty much a ghost town, so there is no worry of intrusion. I know it's just lunch, but these moments with Freddie are sacred.

"How you making out, man? Everything good?"

"It is, Freddie. It really is." There's something I'm dying to tell him, but the moment just doesn't seem right.

"How long's your man in town for?" Freddie asks a question I know he knows the answer to. He knows more about the members than they know about themselves.

"Almost two weeks," I say. I tap my fingers on his desk. "Twelve days, to be exact."

"That's some good money."

"*Real* good. He doesn't hardly play eighteen, but he pays me the same as the other caddies, long as I stick around." I laugh. "Like I got somewhere to go."

"Everybody's got somewhere they'd rather be," says Freddie.

I shake my head. Not me. I like it here just fine.

"How's the book? Coming along?"

"It's coming," I say, referencing the novel I've been working on for four years. I know it'll never see the light of day, but I don't tell that to Freddie. "Not enough hours in the day," I say.

"I thought everybody got twenty-four."

I can't take it another minute, so out it comes. "I shot seventy yesterday, Freddie. At Forest Hills. Remember how windy it was?"

Freddie nods. "I do. It was howling like Wolfman Jack."

"Never even got into the forties," I say. "And neither did I—thirty six, thirty four."

I wait for more but it doesn't come. No matter. I've got plenty to say about it.

"You know how you're always asking me what I'm gonna do with my life and that I can't caddy forever?"

"Yeah, man."

"Well, I'm kinda, sorta thinking of going pro again. Well, not really again. I mean for the first time. I should've given it a shot after college. I was the only guy on the team who didn't."

Freddie stays silent.

He's trying not to give me enough rope to hang myself, but I'm too stupid to realize it.

"So what do you think?"

"About you turning pro? Hell yeah, man. Why not? Never know until you try. Soon as you're shooting in the sixties on your home track every time you tee it up, you'll be ready to take the Nike Tour by storm."

Freddie knows more about my golf game than anybody. I hold the dubious distinction of being Freshman of the Year and Most Improved Senior.

"You want some more?" asks Freddie.

Humble pie? I say to myself, not realizing Freddie's pointing at my empty bowl of chowder. I wish I could say I've lost my appetite, but I haven't. Instead I just laugh, as much at myself as at what Freddie just said.

"The truth doesn't always have to hurt," says Freddie, smiling as he grabs my bowl.

54

CHAIRMAN OF THE BOARD

"You ready for some *real* paper?" asks Bull.

I look up from my newspaper. Falcons lose again.

"I'm always ready for that," I say.

"You're in, Trippstah. You're in the group."

"*The* group? You mean—"

"Chairman of the board, my friend," says Bull. His next words come out slow as a line at Six Flags. "Chairman of the board."

Bull is one of Augusta's best, and he's as smooth as Clark Gable. Bull doesn't get grass on his shoes for less than a hundred bucks. He's also the caddy for a certain Augusta member who also happens to be the club chairman.

This is about as high as the cotton gets.

"Wow," I say. "How?"

"The chairman was asking Freddie about the caddies, you know, like he always does. Who's got game and who can't caddy dead. Then he told Freddie he had him a big-time client coming down to finish a deal he'd been working on for a long time. Krugerrands."

"Krugerrands?" I'm thinking *Lethal Weapon 2*.

"Gold, gold, and more gold," says Bull. "A fifty-million-dollar deal, if it goes down."

"Fifty million dollars? Holy shit." I shake my head. I can't fathom a million beers, much less a million dollars.

"I'm honored," I say. "Truly. Thanks, Bull."

"Don't thank me. Thank Freddie. He made the call. I just let it go through. You know what you're doing out there, my friend. You don't need anybody looking over your shoulder anymore."

"I learned from the best," I say.

"Smartest thing you've said all day." Bull smiles and points to Freddie's office. "C'mon, Trippstah. We gotta go. The chairman has his own time schedule. Can't be late for it."

I spring up and walk with Bull to Freddie's office, where a dozen or more caddies are milling about.

"Aww, Freddie. I wanted that bag."

"C'mon Freddie. I need it more than he does."

"This ain't right, Freddie. I been out here longer than he has."

"Ain't my call, man. Member asked for him, member gets him."

"Member asked for White Boy?"

"Asked for Black Boy, too," says Deal Maker, pushing through the sea of caddies with a bag big as a sarcophagus slung over his shoulder. It's all he can do to stand up straight.

I don't know what stuns me more. That I'm in the chairman's group or that I'm in it with Deal Maker.

"White Boy!" yells Deal Maker, slapping out a handshake. "Gonna get us some big money today."

I feel Freddie's eyes on me. This is not just about big money. This is a chance to make an impression on the richest, most influential man at Augusta National.

There is no telling where this might lead.

Freddie hands me my bag and I don't look down, just grab it and sling it over my shoulder. It almost flies off, light as cotton candy. I put down the bag, thinking surely something's wrong. Then I see the reason for the levity. Women's clubs. First time with the chairman, and I'm caddying for a chick.

You gotta be shitting me.

"It's the guest's wife," says Freddie. "She took up the game so she could spend more time with her husband."

I run my finger across the face of a 5-iron. It's brand new. Not a duff mark on it.

Oy vey. I'm caddying for a beginner.

At Augusta, there are no women's tees. Front of the box is all you get. Suffice it to say that for most women this makes Augusta longer than a bad blind date.

Five holes into the round I'm laughing at the brunt of Freddie's joke. This lady can play!

She's pinning his ears back, the hubby with the pocket full of Krugerrands. Deal Maker is handling him the best his crazy ass knows how, but they're just not clicking. On the green he points left and Deal Maker points right. In the fairway he grabs wood while Deal Maker offers iron. My girl is playing like the 10 handicapper I know she must be, but her sand woes are something to behold. All pail and no shovel.

I see no harm in a quick lesson, so the next time she strays one into the bunker I give her a little instruction.

"Open your shoulders," I say. "Feet and hips, too. And when you grip the club, open the face and *then* grip it. Just like that. Now swing through as hard as you can."

The ball pops out and lands on the green like a butterfly with sore feet. She squeals like a schoolgirl.

There's a second day of this, with my girl drumming her husband like she's John Bonham. On the 7th hole, after she blasts out to ten feet from a crappy lie, the chairman walks over and whispers in my ear. His long drawl is like a needle in the vein from an injection you weren't expecting.

"Is she," he points to my player, "*asking* you for help?"

"Yes, sir."

"Don't." He puffs his cigarette. Smoke curls across my face. "Anymore."

"Yes, sir."

The back nine ends, as do the lessons. I can see my player is happy because she's clipped her hubby once again, but a little confused by my lack of support from Amen Corner and beyond. She doesn't say anything, though. Instead she hugs my neck, thanks me for two great days. I hug back, and let go with pockets empty. No tip, but that's okay. The chairman pays at the window like a horse getting 15-1.

Even so, this doesn't sit too well with Deal Maker. He'd want a tip if he were caddying for Jesus Christ.

"I gave him everything I had, White Boy. Everything. And not so much as a 'Thank you' coming off 18. But tha's all right—I got a little something for him. Here. Hold this for a sec."

I grab the upright casket. It's heavy as guilt.

I'm about to drag the sarcophagus into Freddie's office when Deal Maker returns, his pockets bulging. I think briefly about stopping him, but I don't. I watch in silence as he slides two chicken sandwiches into his man's bag, bones and all. Not the pockets, but where the clubs go.

"He said he only plays a couple times a year. Well, I got me a surprise for him next time he tees it up. All that money and nothing for me. Well, we'll see about that."

Deal Maker walks in Freddie's office and grabs his man's travel bag. In go the clubs and chicken. The grin on Deal Maker's face isn't vicious, more like satisfaction. I don't say a word, thinking Deal Maker probably hasn't had too many satisfying moments in his life. No reason to take this one away from him.

"Get my money from Freddie, White Boy. I'll be down at the caddy house." Deal Maker walks down the hill, a happy hitch in his step.

I look at the bag of Mr. Krugerrand, pregnant with greasy chicken. I can't help but reach for the zipper. Half of me says unzip it. The other half says let sleeping dogs lie. I think of all the money Mr. Krugerrand must have, and how little Deal Maker has.

I walk out the door, leaving Rover to his nap.

55

THE OFFER

Somebody must have headed the chicken off at the pass, or Mr. Krugerrand never played golf again, because nothing comes of Deal Maker's poultry putdown. In spite of my teaching reprimand, I am once again invited to be in the chairman's group. In fact, I've become a regular. It's a damn good gig to have, easily double what you would make caddying for a regular member's group, and sometimes even the Holy Grail.

A tip.

It's an afternoon in April, another Masters in the books. I'm coming off the golf course, sweat dripping down my back. It feels more like July, hot as it is, with the air thick enough to chew. I walk in Freddie's office and rag doll into the chair beside his desk. He's on the phone. The look on his face is one of great interest, like he's trading stocks with the bell about to ring.

"Got him right here, sir. He just walked in the door."

Not realizing he's talking about me, I turn to see who's there.

"Right away. Yes, sir," says Freddie. He cradles the phone and points. "You got a minute?"

I'll always have a minute for Freddie Bennett. On my death bed I'll have a minute.

"Sure," I say. "What's up?"

"On our way, sir," he says, hanging up the phone.

Freddie briefs me on the cart ride over, but I'm still not sure what this is all about.

"You like the chairman? Like caddying in his group? Like his guests?"

"Sure," I say to all three. "He's actually a really nice guy. You wouldn't know he's one of the richest men in the world just by talking to him."

"He likes you, too. A lot. Thinks you've got potential."

"Really?"

I wonder how he determined that from watching me read greens and spout yardages.

"He likes the way you deal with other folks, specifically his guests, and they're almost as high dollar as he is. They've all said good things about you. Believe me when I say he asks every last one of them what they thought of their caddy."

This surprises me. Not that I feel most members couldn't give a damn about their guests' caddies as long as theirs wasn't a grass smasher.

"The chairman wants to talk to you. Man to man," says Freddie. "You okay with that?"

"Sure," I say.

I'd be lying if said I wasn't suddenly nervous. Not first-date shakes, but enough butterflies to fill the net.

Freddie parks the cart and I get out. I hadn't been paying attention to where we were going, fixated as I was on the conversation.

Whoa. What the hell are we doing *here*?

We walk around the cabin, where a white veranda overlooking Ike's Pond is high above us. A man in a tuxedo introduces himself and motions for me to join him. I don't recognize his name, but I recognize him.

The chairman's valet.

I take the steps one at a time, unsure of what is waiting for me at the top. I look over my shoulder for Freddie, even though I know he's no longer there. I try to push the thought from my head, but it is a stone before the tomb, and I am not Jesus.

I cannot roll it away.

"Have a seat," says the imposing figure in the tuxedo. He looks so pressed even his skin seems starched.

"Would you like a Coke?" He stops, looks me in the eye to the point where we are staring. "Beer?"

Though we drink it like sailors from a cooler in the trunk of my car at the end of the day, alcohol is strictly forbidden for the boys in white. A caddy caught drinking on the grounds is a caddy looking for work.

"A Coke would be great," I say.

The valet returns quickly with a glass-bottled Coke and a tumbler filled with ice. He spins it around so the Augusta National logo faces me, staring me down like a vulture. The valet pours the brown liquid over the ice until he seems satisfied it is just the right amount, one finger from the rim. He sets down the bottle, turns, and leaves.

I never see him again.

It feels wrong to be out here, like I'm trespassing on grounds I should never be on even if asked. I push away my Coke.

"Drink it," a voice says. "It's all right. Ain't like nobody put nothing in it."

The body belonging to the voice comes around from behind me and pulls up a chair. He's also wearing a tuxedo, but no jacket. I recognize him. He works in the dining room. Has for many years.

"You want to make some money?"

"Sure," I say.

"*Lots* of money?"

I nod. "Who doesn't?"

"Want to travel the world? Meet people. Eat good. Drink good?"

I'm still nodding.

"You got a wife? Girlfriend?"

"Girlfriend," I say. "Pretty serious."

"How serious?"

"We've been dating for four years. Five years this September."

"Think she'd come with you?"

"Come with me where?"

Whatever this is, it's happening too fast.

"Anywhere. Everywhere. Wherever the chairman's jet decides you need to go."

"You've lost me. Why would the chairman want to fly me and my girlfriend around the world?"

"I'll cut to the chase, caddy." He emphasizes the word caddy. "The chairman wants you to be his new valet."

"His *valet?*"

"Did I stutter?"

It suddenly gets quiet and cold.

"Don't look so proud. You won't be the first white folk to valet for the chairman. Few years back a white couple ran the show. Made a ton of money, but the wife wanted to have kids, so they quit. Moved to Indiana or some such."

"Oh," I say, wishing I could say something else. I realize, too, that the chairman will not be walking out on this veranda unless I say yes. I realize I am being screened.

"How 'bout it, Tripp?"

I half shake my head. I feel dizzy. This has come out of nowhere.

"I don't know. I—can I think about it?"

"Who needs to think about the job of a lifetime? You know how many people would kill for this job?"

On the surface it *is* the job of a lifetime. The only things missing are fast cars and fast women, and I'm not entirely sure they're not.

"I'm sure it's a great gig," I say. "I just need some time. It's a big decision."

"It's an easy decision."

I can tell from the edge on his voice he's just about done with me. I can understand why. Who wants to be the bearer of bad news to the most influential man at Augusta National?

"They shoot the messenger, you know," he says, as if reading my mind.

"I'm sorry," I say, my eyes on my shoes. "I need some time to think about this."

"I don't get what's to think about. Good money. Travel. All that goes with it. You'll live like a king. And all you got to do is lay out the man's clothes in the morning and make sure there's a drink in his hand when the sun goes down."

Time freezes. For how long I don't know.

"It's not the chairman. He's been nothing but nice to me, good to me. It's me, all me. I just need some time to think about it."

"I ain't so sure there *is* time."

I shrug my shoulders so hard it hurts.

"It's the best answer I've got."

The curtains guarding the bay window move just a little, just enough to show someone was there.

"I guess I better go."

"I guess you better." He stares at the Coke in the member's glass with a look that tells me not to touch it, that it no longer belongs to me.

"There's a cart out front. Take it."

"Thanks," I say, and just like that I'm gone.

Minutes later I'm in Freddie's office. The moment I walk in he asks a question he already knows the answer to.

I have a terrible poker face.

"How'd it go?"

"I don't know, Freddie. I don't think I can do it."

The expression on Freddie's face hurts my heart.

"I'm not saying I'm above it or anything. I mean I'm out here, aren't I? It's not like I'm too good to caddy."

The look on Freddie's face says I should quit while I'm ahead. I rub my pants and then my eyes. "I don't know, Freddie. It ain't the chairman, it's me. I just don't think I'm ready for something like this. Taking off and leaving to a world I know nothing about."

Freddie looks at me. Eye to eye, man to man. To my surprise, he's smiling, even though it's obvious he is not happy with my decision.

"Can I have the weekend to think about it?"

"I don't know. He flies out tomorrow. I imagine that job will fly out with him."

That's how *I* feel, I want to say. I'm out of the nest, just not ready to fly.

I never caddied in the chairman's group again.

My fault, not his.

56

THE GORILLA COMES BACK

Not all knowledge is good, and I'm sorry I learned about this.

I'm walking down 11 fairway, the morning air crisp as lettuce and the ground wet with dew. I call these Magic Bags, getting paid for eighteen when you only go nine. Somebody with a plane to catch but they want one last taste of Augusta, even if it's just nine holes. These bags are rare as hen's teeth, and when you get one you never know if it's your last.

It's early, so early the grounds crew is barely beating us, the greens freshly mowed as we reach each tee.

It's so early that I don't notice it at first. A caddy, one of Augusta's best, who can read these greens in his sleep, is holding what appears to be an iron shaft, not three inches long. He lights the bottom and puts his mouth on the middle, breathing in deep like he's toking weed.

What in the hell?

He's not trying to hide what he's doing. Why should he? It's just me and him. The players are back on the tee—no way can they see over this hill.

He comes closer, again lighting the iron shaft with a cupped hand. To block the wind I suppose, although there is none.

"What in the hell is that?" I say.

"What in the hell is what?"

I point.

"Oh, this here?" He says it casually, like everybody's got one. "This here's what's left of a 6-iron. And some screen from my grandmama's porch."

"Your grandmama's porch?" The caddy looks fifty if he's a day. "She's still alive?"

"Yeah, she 'bout ninety-five and change, I reckon. She helped me cut out a piece so I wouldn't make a mess of it."

"You're shittin' me."

"Course I am."

He reaches into his pocket as a ball lands in the fairway some thirty yards from where we're standing. "That would be *your* man," he says, opening a plastic baggy. "He can smoke it, skinny as he is. Looks like a goddamn praying mantis."

He drops what looks like a jagged roly-poly onto the tiny screen covering the top of what's left of the 6-iron's shaft. He puts his mouth on the bottom and lights the middle, sucking in air like a dying man. Which of course, he is. He just doesn't know it.

Or if he does, he doesn't seem to care.

"Po' man's crack pipe," he says. "Pretty clever, ain't it, White Boy?" He spews out the poison, laughing. His eyes look like a relief painting, blood red and bulging.

"Yeah," I say. "Pretty clever."

What the fuck? is what I want to say. *Have you lost your mind?* is another.

He sucks in one last puff, turns to me and smiles.

"Yo, you want a hit?"

* * *

Over lunch in Freddie's office, the Magic Bag jetted off to Seminole, I tell him about my morning. I don't mention any names. Neither does Freddie. We both know what we know.

"That crack's a motherfucker, man. Doesn't care how big you are, how little. You're going down—down to a place where you never get up." He stirs his clam chowder, pushes it away, starts ticking off names with his middle finger.

"I paid for rehab, tried intervention, tried holding their money. But there ain't *no* going back once you cross that crack. Don't you even think about doing it. I know you drop 'em off at the houses. I know how close you get to it."

"No way," I say, shaking my head. "No way in hell. Only thing going up my nose is my finger."

Freddie laughs, but it's not funny.

"This ain't coke, man. This is crack. Two different beasts. Coke is just a monkey on your back. Crack is a goddamn gorilla!" Freddie pounds his desk, something I've never seen before. He walks over to the window with his arms crossed tight against his chest. He looks out the window for a very long time.

His soup gets cold. Not that it matters. Freddie has lost his appetite.

I get up to walk outside. "I gotta run get something. Be back in a minute."

"Yeah, man," he says. His voice sounds deflated, defeated.

Crack is indeed a goddamn gorilla, and this gorilla is breaking Freddie's heart.

57

WELCOME BACK, KOTTER

In the summer of '92 I return to Cuthbert, happy to find a contagious side to the junior golfers I left behind. I was wrong in assuming their enthusiasm for the game would die like leaves on a tree with winter fast approaching. With some of the kids, just the opposite has happened, in particular a young girl named Summer, who I'm told has not missed a day since I left, crappy weather be damned. When I first met her, she didn't even know which end of the club to hold, and now she's breaking 80.

Breaking 80! After just one year.

A lot can happen in a year. I used to believe it could happen to me, too. Maybe it still can.

Summer doesn't have to tell me how much she loves the game. I can see it in her eyes, hear it in her voice, witness it in her early arrival and late departure. She wins my end-of-the-year tournament going away, and when it's time for me to head home she tells me she wants to play college golf and one day go pro.

Summer will one day make good on her desires as a four-year All-American at the University of Georgia before chasing her dream on the Futures Tour. Summer also tells anyone who'll listen that I taught her the game, taught her how to play. I just shake my head. All I did was open the door—she's the one who walked through it.

Freddie's line, not mine.

58

ONE MORE FOR THE ROAD

My return to Augusta for a fourth season meets little fanfare. I still have no idea what I want to do with my life, what to do with the English degree collecting dust in my desk. I'm only twenty-five, but of all my friends, and I've got a bunch, I'm the only one without a real job, though I suppose you could argue caddying is a real job.

I think it is.

I slip on my white jumpsuit, adjust my green hat. Even though it's October it feels like summer forgot to leave. I push up my sleeves and walk to the practice tee. My main member is in town for a ten-day run, though I don't think he knows it's me who will be toting his bag. I told him at the end of last season I was done, through, finis.

Looks like I lied.

When he sees me he yells, "Abner! Well, well. Look at what the cat dragged in."

To this day I don't know why he calls me that. He never bothered to explain and I never bothered to ask. But he pays big at the window and plays a lot of holes, and I genuinely like him. He's still a different duck, but with a good heart, and we get along just fine.

We shake hands and I reach for his 9-iron, wiping off the dirt with a brand new Masters towel.

"How was your summer, Abner?"

"Good. Not long enough, but good."

"I thought you were done with this place," he says, sending a 7-iron soaring at the flag. He's in his seventies, my guy, but he's limber as Gumby and can still play when he gets things rolling.

Now you know where he got his nickname.

I pretend not to hear him.

"I thought you were done, too," says a voice from behind.

The Englishman. He offers his hand and smiles that same shit-eating grin.

"You came back for me, didn't you? I knew you couldn't leave me like this, you bugger, you."

I laugh. "Is it that obvious?"

"I bet you say that to *all* the boys." The Englishman chuckles and pats me on the shoulder. "Good to see you, Tripp. Welcome back."

"Good to see you, too," I say. "One more go, I reckon."

"I should think that would be enough," he says. There is no laughter in his voice this time. His eyes don't leave me.

I wish I had a response, but I don't.

59

MORE FREDDIE-ISMS

Maybe I came back for the show.

Few if any have Freddie Bennett's hold on the King's English. He spins like a silkworm, leaving you with unforgettable visual imagery.

When telling a story about a caddy who reaches into Rae's Creek and pulls out a water moccasin instead of a Titleist, Freddie says, "You shoulda seen him take off. He was running so fast you could shoot marbles on his shirttail."

On seeing a Tour player's wife in desperate need of a cheeseburger: "That girl is lean as a finishing nail."

To the caddy sniffing around the bags that arrived on a Sunday afternoon: "You don't want his bag, man. He's got short arms and deep pockets."

On caddies showing up to work hungover: "Don't tell me you didn't get in that oil last night. Your eyes look like two piss holes in the snow."

When a caddy marveled at Freddie's amazing strength: "I didn't get these muscles playing pinball, man. I work for a living."

When the pro's daughter walks into Freddie's office with her new boyfriend, showing him off like a piece of jewelry and bragging on his blue blood background, Freddie whispers to me: "He ain't fooling nobody. He's so country you could shuck his shit."

To the caddy who tried to slip into a bag that wasn't his: "If you don't let go of that man's bag I'm gonna stick my foot so far up your ass the orthodontist gonna have to cut my toenails!"

To the caddy who asked Freddie what he was going to do over the summer with the golf course shut down: "Close your eyes, man. Tell me what you see. Nothing! And that's exactly what I'm gonna be doing."

And my favorite, told to me by Freddie when he had to quiet down a raucous caddy house of which I was about to be a part: "I just told 'em that if they didn't shut up, I wasn't gonna pay 'em. Man, it got so quiet you could hear a rat pissing on cotton."

A rat pissing on cotton!

I definitely came back for the show.

60

PROMISES KEPT

It's the fall of '92 and my grandfather is dying, but I convince myself he's not. He's a World War II vet with shrapnel in his body, a man who's beaten a fatal heart attack and a wicked case of hepatitis C. He's also the greatest witness to the word of God I know, so I know he's got friends in high places.

Besides, grandparents aren't supposed to die.

I've never had a family member pass away, and when you are shielded this long from the steely hand of death you get very good at denial. I'm in denial, but I have to be. There's only one more good month of caddying before the club slows down for the holidays, and there's rent to pay and gifts to buy and soon it'll be Christmas and—

And what?

My grandfather lives in Atlanta, a two-hour drive from Augusta. Just a hop, skip, and a jump. But like I said, the days here with good money to be made are precious, and I can't afford to let even one slip through the cracks. Besides, I know he'll beat this just like he's beaten everything else. A disease named after a letter ain't taking down Talmadge A. Bowden, Sr. Not happening. Poppa will be just fine. According to my dad, the doctors at Piedmont Hospital are some of the best in the business.

He should know. He's one of the best docs on the planet.

I run this final thought through my head as I zip up my caddy suit. It's time to go. A high-dollar bag awaits.

On the 1st tee we shake hands and make introductions. No practice range for these fellas. They're ready to hit it and get it. Works for me. The faster the better. My man tells me his name is Byron White, which should ring a bell but doesn't, as I don't watch CNN and slept through my political science class. He's an old coot, my player, with rickety knees and a swing meant for a playground.

He's also a supreme court justice. My man failed to mention that bit, and I don't learn who he is until later, when Freddie tells me I'm fired.

Fired.

The single worst word to a caddy's ears. I've never heard it, even when I was first starting out, a grass-smashing bull with horns as big as a loblolly pine.

Just like that, my weekend is over.

Fired.

"For what?" I ask, my mouth open like a fly trap. I'm standing beside Freddie's desk, and I put my hands down to brace myself.

Freddie half shrugs his shoulders. "Just happens sometimes. He said you acted like you weren't into it, like there was somewhere else you'd rather be. No caddy-player chemistry—that kind of thing. He's still gonna pay you. Don't worry about that."

"I don't want money from somebody who just fired me."

Freddie peels off three twenties and slides them over.

"Don't sweat it, man. Ain't a caddy in the yard that hasn't been fired at least once. Took you longer than most."

That almost makes me feel better. Almost.

I slip the Jacksons into my wallet and head for the door. *Fired.* I still can't believe it There's nothing else to do but go home, and so I do.

Yes, I'm back. Back living at home, having come full circle. All of my roommates are married. Me? I've run out of folks to latch onto.

The next morning the phone rings, the sun barely kissing the sky. I answer on the second ring, thinking it must be Freddie, that ol' Byron had a change of heart. But it's not Freddie. It's my dad. My dad, who has been in Atlanta all month, holding a vigil at Piedmont Hospital with his dying father.

Grandparents aren't supposed to die.

"Hello?"

"Tripper. Good morning, son."

Pop almost never calls me son.

"Sorry to wake you."

I start to tell him my alarm was about to go off but then I remember I hadn't set it. No reason to.

"Everything all right?"

"Poppa is very sick. You might want to come up. Don't drive crazy, but I think you need to get here today."

"Sure," I say. "I got today off. Tomorrow, too. I got fired off a bag, Pop. Can you believe it?"

"Yes. I know."

How does he know?

"You do?"

Pop doesn't answer, just tells me to drive safe. I tell him I love him and hang up the phone. I pack light. Only going for a night. The weekend is here and there'll be plenty of high-dollar bags to be had—plenty of high-dollar bags that won't fire me.

Damn you, Whizzer White.

* * *

I don't remember the drive down I-20, don't remember parking my black Trans Am at Piedmont Hospital. But I'll never forget the color of the hospital walls, like the color was once there but had long been removed. I'll never forget how it smelled: not of death, but not of life, either.

More like limbo.

I walk into the waiting room and a favorite cousin hugs my neck before ushering me through double doors. Her face is stained with tears, old and new. As the doors swing behind me, I turn to see my grandmother, slumped against the wall, her pretty face buried in her hands. She looks at me through a stream of tears and disbelief.

I don't remember what she said, but there was no need for words anymore. I knew what had happened. Poppa was gone.

We held each other and cried until we could cry no more.

Talmadge Arton Bowden, Sr., died in his medicated sleep aged 79 years, 8 months, and 4 days. Nine years later my grandmother, Nellie Ruth Bowden, would follow him, also aged 79 years, 8 months, and 4 days.

The Lord works in mysterious ways. So does Freddie Bennett. Freddie is the one who fired me, not Whizzer White.

How he knew the end was near I'll never know.

61

SECOND CHANCE OF A LIFETIME

"So what're you going to do with your life, mate?"

It's a question reserved for Freddie, but this time it's coming from the Englishman, who's back in town for a three-day run. It's not the first time he's asked me. And it's not the first time I answer I don't know.

"What do you know about advertising?" he asks.

"Advertising? You mean like TV commercials?"

"Any and all media. TV, print, radio, outdoor, bus stop kiosks, backlit airport signage, duratrans. You name it."

"I don't know shit about advertising."

"Perfect," he says, switching from a 9-iron to a wedge. "You were born for the job."

"What job?" I say. I have no idea where this conversation is going.

"Copywriter. You said you like to write. You're quick on your feet—you can turn a phrase."

I shrug, nod. "Yeah," I say.

A job? A real job?

"You can't caddy forever, you know."

I know. I think of my last job offer on these hallowed grounds. I should have taken it. It haunts me to this day.

"Where would I work? I mean, where is the job?"

"Where else, friend? New York City. Advertising mecca of the world. There's only one Madison Avenue, you know."

"I'll be working on Madison Avenue?" I say it like I know what the phrase means.

"If it were the 1960s," he says, laughing. "No, our office is on Lexington Avenue—46th and Lexington, in a big building made of glass. Not that I've narrowed it down. Everything in New York is big and made of glass."

"New York City." When I say it out loud, I sound like the cowpoke in the salsa commercial. "Wow. I don't know what to say."

"How about saying yes?"

This time I don't hesitate. This time I do something very uncharacteristic. This time I go for it.

"Excellent," says the Englishman. He slaps me on the back and grabs his putter. "You'll make a brilliant copywriter. Absolutely brilliant. But if for some odd reason you don't, I'll pretend I don't know you." He laughs and pops me on the shoulder.

"Thanks," I say, dumbfounded. I can't believe I'm going to New York. "So, what's the next step?"

"The next step? Yes, sorry. You might need to know that little detail so you can plan your descent upon our lovely city. Augusta closes in May, yes?"

"Third week," I say. "Closing Week. I'm done on Sunday."

"We'll see you then," he says. "When I get back to the office, I'll make the necessary arrangements. It's a done deal, Tripp. It's not like there's a need to interview. I'm comfortable with this hire. I've no doubt you'll do a great job."

And just like that, my caddying days are over.

62

OFF YOU GO

The offer to write copy in New York for the largest ad agency in the world doesn't sink in until later, when I'm sitting in Freddie's office, everyone gone for the day but us.

I wring my hands, rub my knees. I'm twenty-six years old, a grown man, and even though I'm afraid, I'm not afraid to say it.

"It's a little scary, Freddie. What if I screw this up?"

"So what if you do?" he says. "But you won't. I'm sure of it." Freddie puts down his black book and looks at me. "There ain't nothing to be afraid of, man. You can always come home, but you might not get another chance to leave. At least not like this. New York is the big leagues. Chance of a lifetime, man."

How many people get a second chance of a lifetime?

"Tell you what," says Freddie, tossing a magazine into the trash. "You change your mind and want to come home, I'll come get you. How's that sound?"

I smile.

"Sounds like I better start packing."

63

START SPREADING THE NEWS

Freddie was wrong. There's a lot to be afraid of in New York. Franklin Delano Roosevelt was right. There's nothing to fear but fear itself.

When the plane touches the tarmac at LaGuardia International Airport, I'm a jangled mix of nerves and excitement.

They say this city never sleeps, and while I'm here neither do I. I find a one-bedroom apartment on 81st and 3rd that I share with a buddy from back home. It's really just a closet with a stove and toilet, but for now it suits just fine. I have a futon in the corner and a computer by the window. For the first time in my life, I've been hired from the neck up.

True to his word, the Englishman brings me into the intimidating world of big business advertising. McCann Erickson is a Goliath of an agency, with offices all over the world.

International opportunities await.

True to my word, I know nothing of advertising, but I've never been afraid when there's a pen in my hand and I throw myself into my work, eager to become McCann's most dedicated copywriter. I'm hourly with a time sheet, and I fill in the daily boxes with numbers like 8.5, 11.5, 9.75, and 10. I get paid $7.50 an hour, time and a half for anything over forty hours a week.

I also starve to death.

My first introduction to New York City economics is a humbling one. It begins with two Fuji apples, a bag of chips, Marlboro Lights in the box, and a six-pack of tall boys.

I slide the items onto the counter and an Asian man with

a permanent grin taps away at an ancient cash register. He slides the items into two black bags. One for beer and cigarettes, one for food.

"Twenty-three eighty," he says.

My eyes bulge. I've only got a Jackson in my wallet and a credit card with less room than my apartment. Thank God no one's in line behind me.

This is the kind of embarrassment you wear like a duster.

I don't see myself mopping floors or polishing apples to make up the difference, and with my Friday paycheck four days away, I do what any red-blooded American male would do: I tell him to keep the apples and chips.

The Asian gent takes my twenty, returns a few singles and change. I don't bother to count it. I walk out into the New York sunshine, pop a tall boy, and slide in a straw.

The realization is clear: In New York I can drink or I can eat, but I can't do both.

At least not until the Friday paycheck.

I lean against the side of a building so tall it blocks the sun. I sip my beer, cold and refreshing, smiling as the world passes by. As opposed to passing me by. Trust me, there is one hell of a difference.

It may not feel like it, may not look like it, but the wheels of my life are finally in motion.

64

LIFE IN THE BIG CITY

My stay in New York City is a rocket launch from being dull.

A week into my New York adventure, my roommate and I return from the Jersey Shore to find we've been robbed. The crooks came in through the window, snapping iron bars which, according to the cop, "couldn't keep out a high wind much less a thief." An open front door was not what tipped us off, as the thieves were kind enough to lock it on their way out. They stole my computer, printer, Walkman, and four pairs of Levi's jeans, neatly pressed and hanging in my closet. My roommate isn't sure what's missing of his stuff, as his shit is everywhere. I'm equally guilty. When the cop looks around the room and says, "*Jesus*, they did a number on this place!" we laugh like stoners.

We don't last but a few months in our digs on 81st and 3rd, as the building is soon condemned when reports of asbestos in the walls turn out to be accurate. My roommate and I blame the deadly insulation for our continuous coughing, not the cigarettes and smog we ingest into our lungs on a daily basis.

All is not lost, however.

We upgrade to 57th and 6th when my Wall Street roommate talks his Wall Street girlfriend into letting me move in with them. At the time, it sounds like a great idea, at least to me. Sure beats the hell out of being homeless or living at the YMCA.

Turns out it doesn't beat it by much.

The girlfriend and I hit it off like the Three Stooges, and I am soon relegated to sleeping on the floor. She has a pristine white couch that doesn't quite match her perception of my cleanliness, which, shall we say, is not even remotely next to godliness. The apartment is beyond tiny, with a galley kitchen and a closet impersonating a bedroom. I later learn it used to be a hotel and I believe it, because when you sit on the crapper you have to prop your feet on the rim of the tub. But this does not present as much of a challenge to me as it does to my roommate, since the girlfriend quickly grows tired of me invading their bedroom at odd hours of the night (not that I blame her) and soon bans me from bathroom privileges after 9 P.M.

But that's no hill for a climber, and I soon befriend the owner of the all-night deli across the street.

"Not a problem," he says in a New Jersey accent thick as a phone book. "You keep buying from me, you can use the facilities all you want." He points to a door beside the beer fridge, the blue paint peeling like a sunburn. "No lock on it, so keep your foot against the door, you know, when you're in there." He laughs and rubs his big belly. "All the comforts of home."

Which leads me to the night I spend with a homeless man. Percy, I think his name is, but I'm terrible with names. He's standing on a street corner one Thursday evening, handing out coupons to a strip club. I take one and keep walking, but something stops me.

What it was I'll never know. The hand of God? A red light?

I turn around.

"Hey, man. How much you make an hour?"

"For what?"

"For this," I say, holding up the card.

"Ten bucks," he says. "Most times. Sometimes he pays me twenty and says don't come back till they're gone."

"How many you got left?"

He reaches into a brown bag and pulls out a stack of cards. Two hundred? Five hundred? It's impossible to tell.

"I got twenty bucks," I say. "You want a beer?"

"Does a monkey have lips?"

I laugh and take that as a yes, a yes that leads to an introduction with Percy and the deli owner, who agrees to let Percy use the facilities anytime, provided I'm still holding up my end of the agreement.

Spending the night with Percy on the streets of New York, where I learn the art of eating out of trash cans (you would be surprised what all is in there), throwing up behind a building (for this I needed little training), and panhandling, although we only do that briefly, as I just got paid and money, if only for the moment, is not an issue.

My night with Percy ends with the sun coming up, and me running back to my apartment to get him a starched white shirt with a Henley collar, a pair of tennis shoes, and socks. Percy thanks me and I wish him luck, tell him he knows where to find me, and if I can ever do anything to help him I will.

I never see Percy again.

I do, however, see Yogi. Every night, like clockwork.

Yogi is a homeless man from New Orleans who's lived in New York for over twenty years. He plays a mean trombone (at least I think that's what it is—me, I can only play the radio), his favorite tune being *When the Saints Go Marching In*. I always toss some change into his Cool Whip tub, and he lets me dance along while he plays and sings. People stop and stare; at him, at me, I don't know. Nor do I care. On Fridays I make it a dollar and an Arizona iced tea. Yogi is the rarest of homeless men—a reformed alcoholic who no longer drinks or does drugs of any kind. He tells me the streets saved his life, and though that may sound crazy to you, it makes perfect sense to me.

Especially when I hear Yogi play:
Oh, when the saints go marching in,
Oh, when the saints go marching in,
Lord, how I want to be in that number
When the saints go marching in!

I've been back to New York a number of times since my stint as an ad man, and every time, I look for Yogi. I never find him. I don't know if he's moved on, died, or what. But I do know this, and I know it deep, deep, deep down in my heart:

I know he's in that number.

65

YOU CAN AND YOU WILL

My New York run ends on the Jersey shore, holding hands with a native New Yorker who works on Wall Street. A bond broker, of all things. Her mom is pure Alabama, born and bred, her dad first-generation Italian. This makes for a very interesting woman, and I don't just mean the green eyes and olive skin.

The relationship with my girlfriend of seven years has dissolved like a tablet in water; nobody's fault but our own, though if you had to point a finger you'd probably point it at me.

I push the thought from my head and dig through the brown sand for more sea glass. In the South we hunt for sharks' teeth. Up North it's sea glass, bits of broken bottles worn smooth by the ocean's ways.

Who would have thought a shattered Michelob bottle could be as beautiful as a sunset?

"Wow, take a look at this one," I say, holding up a piece of sea glass as big as my thumb. It's the color of amber. I angle a ray of sunshine off her pretty brown face.

"Don't leave," she says, even though she knows I have to go.

"We promised not to talk about it, remember?"

"*You* promised. I never said such a thing."

She's right. She didn't.

She's ten years older than me, but that's not what is making me go. I have a job lined up in Atlanta, writing copy for a public relations firm with clients like Andre Agassi and Evander Holyfield. They're waiting on me. It's time to do what I was born to do.

"You can stay at my place. Finish that book you're always talking about. I can pay the bills while you work on the great American novel." She puts a hand on my cheek, the same hand that gave me comfort when no other hand did.

"I know it'll be great. I just know it."

I can't lie, can't say these words don't hurt my heart, but those are commitments you make with someone you love, and that's just not how I feel. A circle will never be a square, no matter how many times you draw it.

I look into her eyes, green with amber specks, much like the color of the sea glass balanced in my hand. This would be one of those lifetime moments if I changed my mind and said yes.

Yes. Yes, I'll stay.

But as much as I love it here and almost love her, New York just isn't for me. Kinda like rap music wouldn't have been for Elvis, even if he got his groove on.

I could never call New York home.

I have to go, and I have to go now.

66

EXODUS

Walking into Freddie's office is like walking back in time.

It's not all that big, but it's open, like a loft apartment. Against one wall is an old chest-style refrigerator freezer, like the kind you see in country stores, made of metal, with sliding glass doors so you can reach in and grab what you need. Freddie keeps a little bit of everything in there, from frozen pompano to the catch of the day. There's always the little eight-ounce Cokes, so cold it hurts your teeth to drink one.

Against another wall are members' bags, past and present. They're in no particular order—*scattered* might be a better word— though Freddie knows exactly whose bag is where. During the Masters the players' bags are mixed in with the members' bags, which I've always thought was as cool as Fonzie. I bet the members think so, too.

You can access Freddie's office two ways. From the alley between the pro shop and tournament headquarters, off a little cement pathway that leads to the caddy house. Or from inside the pro shop, through a small hallway that leads to the storage room chock-full of extra shirts and bag towels.

The desk Freddie sits behind is big but welcoming, just like him, with lots of miles on it. It's no surprise he keeps it neat, with just an ashtray and the Black Bat holding court. A little black-and-white TV comes out during the Masters, but that's about it. In the top drawer you'll find the big stack of bills he uses to pay the caddies.

A few odds and ends like pencils, pens, rubber bands. His black book is in there, too.

In a bottom drawer is a calendar with scantily-clad ladies, if you can call a birthday suit "scantily clad." Folks come in asking Freddie what day it is, his cue to hand them the calendar. One old guy always says, "Boy, Freddie. I sure do love November," no matter what month it is, before flipping to the page with Miss November.

What's not to love?

Just outside Freddie's door sits a little black hibachi. It's not unusual to see Freddie firing it up at lunchtime, grilling kielbasa or brats, dousing them with mustard and eating them straight from the fire.

On the other side of the pathway is the bag drop. It's really just a long wooden lean-to, with dowels sticking out to separate the bags. It's painted green, of course.

It's also gone.

* * *

It's the Masters following my stint in New York, and I've said the five magic words to slip beyond the yellow ropes and into the office of the man responsible for making it all happen.

I've come to say thank you.

Except I can't. I'm so stunned by Freddie's new office I can't even speak, can't even answer his simple question.

"So tell me about New York, man. How was it?"

Freddie's new office. I never thought I would live to see the day.

I look around. This is not an office; this is an oversized cubicle, with two big windows and a door that opens from the waist up so the bottom half stays closed and the top half open, so someone walking by can see in or hand Freddie something or damned if I know what.

I'm in a daze. This is wrong.

Bags are now stored in the back of Freddie's office, in what could pass for a giant lazy Susan except instead of going round and round it moves side to side, making one hell of a racket. Gone is the old freezer, Freddie's old desk, the hibachi grill.

Gone is everything that made his old office so special.

The old office had more personality than a family reunion. This one is completely devoid of it, as if it's been removed, like you would a wart or a mole.

"What happened to your office, Freddie?" It's all I can manage to say.

Freddie rubs his hands on the new desk. He looks at me before speaking.

"Ecclesiastes, man. There's a time and a purpose for everything. And soon it'll be time for me to move on. I ain't no spring chicken anymore."

Ecclesiastes? Spring chicken?

"What are you trying to say, Freddie?"

"I'm saying I ain't the Caddy Master anymore. Augusta's gone big business, man. Caddy house belongs to someone else now. Had to happen sooner or later."

"Tell me you're joking," I say. "How can you not be the Caddy Master of Augusta National? That's like taking Walt's name off Disney World."

Freddie slides a name tag across his desk. I pick it up.

"'Club Director of Outside Personnel'? What the hell does that mean?"

"It means I'm still part of the team."

Still part of the team.

This should make me feel better but it doesn't.

67

STYROFOAM CUPS

Freddie and I stay in touch over the years, but I let life get in the way. With the exception of Masters Week and Christmas, I seldom see the great man. I have a life now—a pretty good one—thanks to Freddie's behind-the-scenes magic. One day I'm going to thank him for it.

One day.

Much has happened since I left the caddy yard. New York was a life-changing success, leading me to start my own advertising agency with a partner who has the gift of gab and a knack for public relations. We call our agency Seeing Eye Dog Advertising, after the short story by Ernest Hemingway. I like the name, like what the name implies. Too much blind-leading-the-blind in this business.

I said goodbye to apartment living and bought a house in Atlanta with my magical fiancée, a childhood sweetheart who has once again stolen my heart, although I'm not sure she ever let go. I certainly never let go of hers.

I live on a canopied street near Piedmont Park with grand old oaks and towering loblollies, just like at Augusta National. Trust me when I say that helped bring me closer to the closing table.

We're engaged to get married, Fletch and I, in October of this year. Halloween, of all days. We'll have fourteen bridesmaids, twenty-seven groomsmen, zero wedding directors. We'll serve prime rib and Krystal burgers, and float eight kegs of beer.

We're paying for the wedding, so if you think we're leaving early, leaving you behind to revel in our moment and drink us out of house and home, think again.

You better pour one up for me. *And* my bride.

But that's six months away.

I almost have to look at a calendar to believe the date: April 13, 1998. Masters Sunday. How could that much time have gone by? So much has changed, but one thing has not, and I pray it never will.

I can still say those five magic words, and they work just like they did when I was a ten-year-old kid.

I'm here to see Freddie.

* * *

"Hey, man. Who's this good-looking thing you got with you? She looking for the lost and found?"

I laugh. "Just found," I say, shaking Freddie's hand. "Freddie, this is Kim Fletcher, my fiancée. I call her Fletch."

She leans in to give Freddie a hug.

"Fletch? As in *the* Fletch? That pretty young thing from ninth grade? The one that made you miss all those putts?"

Freddie forgets nothing.

Fletch smiles. "It's nice to finally meet you, Freddie. Tripp has told me so much about you."

"I'm afraid most of it's true," he says, laughing as he sits down in his chair. He offered it but Fletch declined.

Freddie reaches across his desk and turns down the volume on the ancient black and white.

"There's your winner," he says, pointing to the golfer standing on the 16th tee. "Go ahead and fit him for the Green Jacket."

Mark O'Meara? The closest he's ever come to winning a major is a friendship with Tiger Woods.

"*That* guy?" I say. "What about Duval? Couples?"

Freddie shakes his head. "Not this year, man. Today is O'Meara's day." He taps a thick finger on his desk.

"But O'Meara's two back with three to play."

"One of those things you just know, man. Don't know how, don't know why. You just do."

I can't help but smile. One of the things you just know. It's been twenty years since I first sat down at Freddie's desk, and there have been a hundred years of changes since. It's nice to know at least one song remains the same. I'm not a betting man, but I bet Freddie's right.

When O'Meara knocks what looks to be a 6-iron onto the green, I pull what is definitely a silver flask from my pocket. Since the day I turned twenty-one, I've wanted to share a drink with Freddie. Hard to believe we never have. We've broken bread many times, but never the seal.

"Hey, Freddie. Care for a taste?" I dangle the flask over his shoulder, a carrot to a horse, blocking his view of the TV.

Freddie shakes his head. "Naw, man. I quit drinking. Doctor's orders."

"It's Crown Royal," I say.

"Oh," he says, handing me a Styrofoam cup. "I didn't stop drinking *that*."

68

EMPTY WINDOW

Freddie retires in the year 2000, and that year's Masters is truly his last. His retirement is just a formality, sad as that is to say. The caddy yard was never the same once CaddyMaster Incorporated took over, virtually handcuffing one of Freddie's greatest assets: the assigning of caddy and player. How Freddie did it, "teaming" is the word I'd use. Sure, a member with pull can still get his favorite caddy, but the rest of the pairings are pure lottery, a roll of the dice. Luck, if you will.

Bad luck, if you ask me.

No longer can Freddie do what no one does better—match the right caddy to the right personality, or help a caddy down on his luck by assigning what we call a good bag—a member who pays big at the window or a guest who drops it like it's hot. Gone, too, are the days of cash on the barrelhead, when an Augusta National caddy was considered a cash advance on a member's bill.

Uncle Sam comes calling these days, because caddies are now salaried, same as you and me.

I'd like to say I made it by to see Freddie for one last Masters, but I can't because it's not true. I tell myself I'm too busy, but that's not true either. More like I don't know what to say. It's not right that Freddie has to go.

Seventy ain't that old. I can imagine what Freddie would say to that.

Not my decision, man. Father Time's. People say it's Mother Nature you should be scared of. They're wrong. It's Father Time that's swinging the hammer that hurts the most.

I later learn Augusta National gave Freddie a pretty decent retirement package, including lifetime Masters tickets and parking passes. But Freddie never once sets foot on the grounds of Augusta National again. The place he called home for over fifty years suddenly becomes as foreign as a third world country.

As if it never even existed.

He tells my dad, "I appreciate what they did for me, I really do, but you know me, Doc. When I'm through, I'm through."

* * *

In the fall of that year my cell phone rings. It's Pop, so I answer. He seldom calls, but when he does there's usually a very good reason.

"Hey, Pop."

"Tripper, my man. What's shakin'?"

"Same ol', same ol'. Stomping out ignorance and superstition every chance I get."

One of Pop's favorite lines. Mine, too.

"Guess what?"

"I'm written out of the will."

He laughs. "No, but now that you mention it . . . "

Now I'm laughing.

"Freddie got inducted."

It sounds like *ab*ducted.

"What? Who the hell would kidnap Freddie?"

"What?"

"You said Freddie got abducted."

"You're getting a new cell phone for Christmas, fruit of my loins. I said Freddie got *in*ducted. To the Caddy Hall of Fame. Class of 2000."

"Ohh," I say. "Thank God. Wow. That's impressive." I say these words not knowing there was such an animal. After a little research, I realize it's a *very* big deal. All the greats are in there, caddies to Caddy Masters. Pappy Stokes, Angelo Argea, Killer Foy—too many to list.

"You should give him a call," says Pop. "I know he'd love to hear from you."

I run some numbers in my head. I haven't spoken to Freddie since 1998, the year I got married. How can that be? I invited him to the wedding, would've asked him to be a groomsman but didn't want to put him in the awkward position of telling me no. There aren't many things in life Freddie doesn't like, but these are at the top: crowds, attention, and having his picture taken.

And that's when I remember. Freddie didn't come to our wedding.

"Tripper? You there? Damn digital cell phones. At least with analog you knew when you were about to lose somebody."

I can tell he's about to hang up.

"I'm still here, Pop. Sorry, my mind was wandering. Hell getting old." I fake a laugh.

"Wait'll you get to be my age, Smoke. When you can't remember where you live or what you were just talking about." There's a pause. "What the hell *were* we just talking about?"

"Freddie. Getting *ab*ducted."

Pop has a great laugh, booming and warm, and he lets one ride.

"I remember now. I was telling you to call Freddie and congratulate him. He'd love hearing it from you. Let me give you his number."

"Got it," I say. "In my cell phone."

"Well, aren't you fancy? I'm lucky if I can turn the damn thing on."

"Stick to surgery and golf," I say.

Pop's handicap was once a two. Now it's ten. He laughs and says he needs eighteen.

"I'll stick to surgery," he says. "Those are wounds I can heal. All right, Tripper, gotta run. Time to head over to the Miracle College and see if I can't perform one or two."

"Sounds good, Pop. Thanks for the call. That's great news. Awesome news."

"My pleasure. Call Freddie, okay? Don't forget."

"I won't. I love you, Pop."

"Love you, too."

We hang up and I scroll through my phone, looking for Freddie's number. It's been two years since we spoke—hard as that is to believe—but congratulations on induction into the Caddy Hall of Fame sounds like a mighty fine icebreaker.

I find the number, punch the key. It hits me before I can even put the phone to my ear. This number I've dialed is the Black Bat, the old rotary phone that sat on Freddie's desk for all the years I've known him.

The Black Bat. Where this story began.

I end the call, lay the phone on my desk, and walk over to my office window, a window not unlike the one Freddie stared out of many a time, watching over his caddies, his flock, his kids.

Only this time there's nothing to see.

69

DARKNESS FALLS TODAY

It's Christmas, 2006, and I have a daughter. Her name is Arrie B. and she just turned two. She can't get enough of this fellow called Santa Claus, can't wait for him to visit.

"Wha's he gon' bring, Daddy? In big sack."

"Love," I say. "And lots of it."

"Love?" she asks. "Wha 'bout Elmo?"

My phone rings. Saved by the cell.

I put a finger to my lips and she turns her attention to Sesame Street. She's a good kid, my Arrie B.

I check the caller ID. It's Pop. Must be calling to wish me a Merry Chris—

"Hello, son."

Pop never calls me son on the first hello.

"Hey, Pop."

There's a pause on the other end, big as the Grand Canyon.

When it comes to death, my dad has seen it too many times to count. It is woven into his very being, like a logo on a shirt. I can't always see it on his face, but I can hear it in his voice, a skill I learned the hard way. A Christmas day, when a kid from Thomson drove his three-wheeler through a barbed wire fence while we were opening presents.

Pop was on call.

Cut the kid in half.

I was hiding on the steps when Pop got home, hoping to surprise him. It was still Christmas Day, after all.

"I lost him," he told my mother.

I left the steps and crawled under the covers. Couldn't tuck 'em in tight enough.

I lost him. Not we, *I*.

Now, another Christmas. On the phone, Pop says, "How are things, Tripper?"

"Good, Pop. Busy, but good."

"Arrie B. asleep?"

"Almost naptime, but not quite. She's right here, watching Sesame Street. Elmo's World. Why? What's up?"

Something is wrong, very wrong.

"Freddie died. This afternoon. He'd fallen a week or so ago. In the kitchen, no big deal at first—but then it went downhill pretty fast." Pop's voice is cracking.

Time freezes. So do I.

"Tripper?"

"Oh, Jesus." It's all I can think of to say.

"I know, son. I know."

"When's the funeral?" I say these words as I collapse into the couch.

"Wednesday."

My heart is in my shoes. I think I'm going to be sick.

"How—how did he die? How do you die from falling in your kitchen?"

Pop explains Freddie's passing to me in layman's terms, but I'm not listening anymore. My mind is on other things. A blue Buick station wagon, an Igloo cooler full of fish, breaking 50 for the very first time.

"You okay, Tripper?"

"Yeah," I say, lying. "So, the funeral, the funeral is Wednesday?"

"That's what they're shooting for. The family wants to move things along. Understandably so."

"Yeah, I can see why." That's not true. I have no idea why.

"Freddie was a good man," says Pop. "They broke the mold on him."

"Freddie was a great man," I say. "There will never be another."

"Yes, sir," says Pop, and the line goes quiet. Neither of us knows what to say.

"I gotta run, Tripper."

"Yeah, Pop. Me, too. Thanks—thanks for calling."

"I knew you'd want to know. Y'all had a pretty special relationship."

"You, too," I say.

"That was Freddie," says Pop. "He had a way of making everybody feel special."

"Even when you weren't," I say, and we laugh, knowing tears are on the way.

"Take care, Pop."

"You, too, Smoke."

"I love you."

"Love you, too."

I hang up the phone and stare at my shoes. I start to cry. On a forty-inch TV, I see Elmo dancing to a beat only he and my little girl can hear.

Me, all I hear is silence, silence in a room so quiet you could hear a rat pissing on cotton.

70

THE ONLY WAY I KNOW HOW

"Not enough hours in the day," I say to an empty room.

I look at my mile-long to-do list. The creative projects have come in fast and furious, with Christmas just around the corner. This client needs a Web site, that client needs a radio spot, this client needs a full-page ad.

I need to be two people at once.

Freddie's funeral is Wednesday, just two days away. I don't see how I can make it. There are too many deadlines hanging over me like bats in a cave, and trying to find a sitter for Arrie B. on such short notice, and Fletch is working full-time and there's just no way to make this happen.

These are lies, of course. It would be another lie to say I'm not a funeral person. I am. In fact, I've done many a eulogy. They are an unforgettable way to say goodbye. Imagine the one I could do for Freddie. The stories I could tell if I could just make it past the tears.

But I don't want to say goodbye, and I'm not going to any funeral. It's not like Freddie would know I wasn't there. He's dead, for Christ's sake.

Man, I know everything.

I hope he knows why I just can't bring myself to go.

71

LOOK HOMEWARD, ANGEL

"Hey buddy. Time to go."

A security guard in a white pickup truck snaps his fingers and points to the iron gate. He's told me twice, but I haven't heard until now. He's smoking a cigarette; I watch as the ash falls to the ground. A Marlboro Red. I can tell by the color of the butt. Same brand Freddie used to smoke.

"Gotta lock up," he says. "Winter hours, y'know?" He points his cigarette at the arrangements and then at me. "Musta been a hell of a guy. Ain't never seen so many people at the graveside before. He a celebrity or something?"

"Something," I say.

More like something else.

I look beyond the gate as the guard drives away. Freddie's blue station wagon is still parked in front of his house; I half expect him to walk out the door and crank it up.

I look at his house and then his grave. Freddie is buried just a sand wedge from the place he called home for over forty years. Imagine your final resting place being just a few doors down from where you raised your kids, loved your wife, welcomed strangers, comforted friends.

With mud-caked fingers I adjust the golf ball one last time, so the inscription "World's Greatest Story Teller" is easily read.

I should have written "Editor."

Freddie didn't tell the story of my life.

He rewrote it.

Of all the things he taught me, these stick out the most: It's never too late to show your appreciation, never too late to make a wrong situation right.

It's never too late to say "thank you."

I grab a clump of dirt and stick it in my pocket, pull a rose from the chairman's arrangement and lay it on a random grave, one that doesn't have any flowers. I can feel Freddie's spirit, strong and vibrant, even in death. His voice is in my ear, and I know that it never really left.

That Thomas Wolfe cat was wrong, man. You can always go back home.

I promise Freddie I will.

72

COUNTING TO FIVE

I make good on that promise.

One year after Freddie's death I move my family back to Augusta, bringing new life to an old house with good bones. The familiar brick street leading to our home still rattles my fillings. I find it comforting, strange as that may sound.

For the first time since the babies came along we all have our own rooms. Our new house is not big, nor is it modern, but it is right where we need to be.

Our backyard is fenced in, perfect for kids and puppies. It backs up to a reservoir, which I take as a very good sign. I'm looking at it now, from the little wooden desk where I write these words. My office in the back of the house is more like a stoop that's been screened in. A bare bulb hangs above, lighting these pages. Indoor-outdoor carpet welcomes my feet.

The carpet is green, of course.

I like it back here, feeling akin to a certain fellow named Stephen King, who I'm told wrote *Carrie* in the laundry room of his single-wide trailer, a typewriter balanced on his knees. Pretty good company if you ask me.

My little girl just walked in, wearing a princess dress and ballet slippers.

"Count to five, Daddy. Count to five."

Four-year-old-speak for "Let's play hide and seek."

I look into her big blue eyes and smile. How lucky I am to have the chance to raise my family just five minutes from where I grew up, less than ten from where I learned about golf and the game of life from a most unlikely teacher.

That teacher is home. And now, so am I.

ACKNOWLEDGMENTS

A shout-out big as the Grand Canyon to my wife Fletch for her unwavering belief in *Freddie and Me*, for her gift in knowing when to kiss my cheek or kick my ass to keep the book moving along, and for working like a rented mule to make sure there was food on the table and toilet paper on the roll while I chased the dream. Guess what, my love? We caught that mother! This book doesn't happen without you. But you know that.

You know everything.

To everyone who took time out of their busy lives to read a rough-as-a-three-day-hangover version of *Freddie and Me* (the version Stephen King defines as "the story undressed, standing up in nothing but its socks and undershorts"), I appreciate your feedback, input, and genuine "Man, I truly believe you can do this" support more than you'll ever know—Fletch, Big E and Jenn, Prince of Tides, Bev, Ray B., Pop and Mimi, Hot Shot and Sweet Pete, Chang and Peter, Cuz Kathy and Hubby Tim, Miz Pickett and Brendan, Gaff, Bobby and Wendy, Erin and Stephen, Texas, Stacy the Wicked Wordsmith, Jan B., Payton, Brandi, Jshizzle, Flint, Monk, Rich, Loi, Rockin' Robin Rosenfeld and Hubby Mark, The Family Haygood (miss y'all) and my dear old friend Kennoy, who wrote the first review on Amazon.

Did I forget anyone? Anyone? Bueller?

Thank you T, for spreading the word of *Freddie and Me* all across the Southeast, to Scott for covering Beijing, to Carla, Paul, Brandon, and Cayte for the rest of the U-S-of-A, and to Corey for your Web site wizardry and Photoshop magic. Check's in the mail. Cash it quick or next time I hire Bessie! Thank you Flint and all the talented folk at Wierhouse for an idea that should've flown, to Kanto for typing all those college short stories without complaint and in lieu of money, and to Wallyburger, for the Pepto Bismol and the wonderful sketching of Augusta's tempestuous layout.

A double thank you to my writing teachers Mrs. Beaird, Naomi Williams, the late Brisco Merry, Tom Bird, and my writing mentor Dr. Walter Evans. Same to Stephen King and Mitch Albom for being so insanely good at what they do (I read *Tuesdays*, *The Shining*, and *For One More Day* over and over during the writing of *Freddie and Me*—brilliant work, those.)

Should have said this sooner, but a special thank you to Pop for doing his best Rod Tidwell impersonation (or maybe it's Jerry Maguire—need to think on that one) and to Jote, Tone, GF, Super Cher, Big E, Jenn and the collective grandparents for watching our two little monkeys with time running out of the hourglass like underage drinkers in a raided speakeasy, so *Freddie and Me* could strap on rollerblades and roll to the finish line. I also want to thank Dr. Gregg Steinberg for jumpstarting the idea—who knew advice over egg salad sandwiches at the Masters would lead to this?

A special thank you to Johnny Johnny for your unconditional friendship and truly magical connections. Everybody may love Raymond, but not near as much as they love you. Another very special thank you to my agent John Andrisani, who, along with my editor Mark Weinstein, believed from the beginning that this was a story that needed to be shared. (I hope every writer who dreams of days like this gets the chance to say things like "My Editor" and "My Agent") Thank you, thank you, thank you, MWW, for dressing *Freddie and Me* in her Sunday best. Your patience and understanding of the craft of putting pen to paper and fingertips to keyboard made this the book it was born to be. And to the wonderful staff at Skyhorse Publishing, thank you for rolling the dice on a craps table like me. Snake eyes, here we come!

To my caddy brothers at Augusta National Golf Club, thank you for welcoming me as one of your own, for taking me under your collective wing, for giving me a place to call home and a purpose in life when I desperately needed one. I'll never forget that, nor will I ever forget you. And for the cherry on top of the sundae of a lifetime, I thank you for teaching me what it means to say, "You gotta rooooollll widdit!"

I yell it to this day.

And to those who took the time to read the story of a most unlikely friendship that spanned some thirty years and knew no boundaries, thank you. I can't help but wonder: Who was the Freddie in *your* life?

Perhaps one day we'll meet and you can tell me.

As for the Freddie in my life, I could never thank him enough for all he did for me, for others, for the game of golf and the game of life. But he knows that.

Freddie knows everything.

My last thank you is to God. It's true, you know. With God all things are possible. You're holding the proof in your hands.

Dream big.